Teacher of the Year

by

Joe David

Library of Congress Catalog Card Number: 96-85521

ISBN 0-939360-03-9

Limited First Edition. Printed in the United States of
America. Published by Books For All Times, Inc.,
Alexandria, VA.

The interview, "Hamme on Education" by Joe David,
published by *Education in Focus* in 1996, has been adapted
from *Teacher of the Year.*

Artwork by
Malone A. Samuels

Books For All Times, Inc.
P.O. Box 2
Alexandria, VA 22313
http://www.bfat.com
TM

*He who has done his best for his own
time has lived for all times.*
— Schiller

In memory of my parents
for their wisdom, kindness, and generosity

The decent docent doesn't doze;
He teaches standing on his toes.
His student dassn't doze and does,
And that's what teaching is and was.
David McCord
What Cheer

One

To think that I, Frank Hamme, with my *pure* English blood must be forced to endure this.

It's unforgivable!

Here I am the most *illustrious* man in the city, personally chosen to teach the best at Horace Mann High, a school the President of the United States created to symbolize the new Renaissance in education, and all I get out of these seniors is indifference.

Why do I remain here when there's a world out there eager to receive me? My direct link to the Earl of Suscrofa makes me the most *desirable* social contact in America. Yet I stay. Is it because I am first and foremost a teacher? Is that why I hide my ancestry and only wear my coat of arms in public on my underpants? I guess deep down beneath my layers of good breeding is a Hamme *born* to teach!

You would think these seniors would realize this. Placing my degrees and coat of arms on the classroom wall, as any respectable professional would do, should be enough to let them know. But my sacrifice to be here, instead of among my own, doesn't impress them. It hasn't yet registered in their *minuscule* brains that I—an English aristocrat and scholar—do them honor to be here, and that my knowledge, acquired at America's *best* schools, can free them of their mental poverty. All I expect is for them to open their minds. The rest I'll do through the magic of teaching.

But instead of opening their minds, they close them the moment I speak.

Some of my wisest remarks, ignored, *not even a frown!* All I get is an empty stare, which only fills with life, when, sitting on the edge of my desk, I spread my legs in celebration of my manhood. It is a relief to note that at least then it is possible to communicate with these 17-year-old half-wits!

Like the true professional that I am, I seize this opportunity before it vanishes and use it to prepare them for a new and important view of life. While thrilling them with my magnificent maleness, I cram their addle brains with literary tidbits on such fascinating teenage topics as incest, necrophilia, and sadomasochism.

As they stare at me in awe, I tell them the story about the homophobic Athenians who destroyed Socrates with guilt and shame because of his pederastic love; I then follow it with some documented remarks about Orwell's lustful fixation on bestiality, which culminates eloquently in *Animal Farm* with: "All animals are equal, but *some* animals are *more* equal than others."

But I am my most brilliant when I quote from my thesis, *Sex in Shakespeare,* and talk at length about Hamlet's exquisite insight into life ("To be or not to be") by underscoring an often overlooked fact: Hamlet's profound love and need for Ophelia.

"Within all of Shakespeare's plays (as within life itself) you must *cherchez la femme!* Hidden somewhere in the corners of each story, there is always a love interest. In poor Hamlet's case, his downfall was the sweet Ophelia. His profound passion for her was so out of control that he did the only thing he could do: *He threw the wench out!* The absolute highpoint theatrically in this great play was when he commanded her to 'Get thee to a nunnery.' Last year when the senior class did the play, and Igor Ivanovich—who has gone on to do some really exciting art films, which you can catch at your favorite adult bookstore—well, when Igor delivered those lines, there wasn't one person in the audience who had doubts about the cause of Hamlet's torture. Just remember always, in literature as in life, *cherchez la femme.* Buried somewhere in the depths of the story, hidden within the clever syntax is always a woman or, for the female writer, a man. Love is what makes the world go round and round and. . . ."

During that period, when every eye was alert to my manhood, as I danced back and forth over hundreds of years of literature, I became the center of their universe, their mover of great ideas. During that period, while filling the room with my intellectual ejaculations, the hymenal-rending cries of virgins, opening their minds to life, were heard ringing gloriously in the air. Even the boys could be heard, sharing expletives, as my male splendor painfully reduced them to the adolescent specks that they were. Yet despite the pain my male splendor caused them, they still listened thoughtfully to my every word. By opening the girls' eyes to the realities of life, I was making the boys' mission easier. In fact, their breathing grew heavy, their pants swelled, as I crystallized with vivid examples the purpose of life: *"Gettin' it on!"*

During that period, while opening their minds to life, I became uncomfortably aware of a girl staring at me, as though she were convinced I was totally mad. The girl, who looked uncomfortable in a modern classroom, resembled an anachronism, a Victorian virgin, shocked easily by any reference to sex.

You would think after taking all those wonderful sex education courses, in which copulating was discussed with such integrity, that by now she would be ready for a *real* education. But judging from my observations of her (and this group in general), it was apparent that she was totally unprepared. Obviously her other teachers weren't doing their job.

Oh, how I miss last year's seniors. Now that was a group with real insight into human behavior. That essay by Tom Wong on the subliminal sexual focus in John Stuart Mills' *On Liberty* was brilliant. I don't think I'll ever forget it, particularly that part in which he sums up his thesis. ("John Stuart Mills' preoccupation with freedom is a thin disguise for his profound need for sexual expression. Throughout *On Liberty*, there are subliminal references to this point, which reach an exciting conclusion in his statement, 'Liberty consists in doing what one desires.'") When I shared his essay with the faculty, there wasn't one teacher who wasn't speechless by this new insight.

Well, I guess I'll just have to work on this class, introduce them to Ovid, maybe some of those romantic poems by Catullus, and that wonderful book by Choderlos de Laclos. It would be so nice if their other teachers were as conscientious as I. It would free me a little, and give me more time to provide them with the finesse they'll need to face that exciting new world out there. I *must* mention this at the next faculty meeting.

Now about that girl. What on earth am I going to do about her?

"Miss Borczyska," I said, when the class was leaving. "May I talk to you?"

"Of course, Mr. *Hammy*," she said, emphasizing the "E" in my name.

"Miss Borczyska!" I said indignantly. "The 'E' is silent."

"Mr. Hamme," she said without the "E." "My name is Borlinda Borgia."

"But your permanent record has your name as. . . ."

"It's *Borlinda Borgia!*" she said, correcting me. "We changed it after the Italian branch of the family."

"You aren't related to Lucrezia?" I asked, impressed.

"No, Mr. Hamme. But on the Catholic side of the family, to a 19th Century pope."

It fits. No real Borgia would ever appear in public looking like her. She was so plain without even any lipstick or rouge for coloring, just a simple high-neck dress (which, I had to admit, despite its looseness revealed a stunning pair of breasts). And the way she carried herself, the way she walked. There was no swing, no girlish tease to it. She moved like a nun out of habit.

God, has this one been neglected!

"You wanted to talk?" she asked, getting directly to the point.

"I most certainly do. It concerns your attitude during my lecture. Did I say something to startle you?"

"You certainly did."

"Would you like to be more specific?"

"I wouldn't know where to begin."

"Anywhere will do."

"Very well," she said. "First of all, Socrates was anything but guilt-ridden about his homosexuality. And *Animal Farm* isn't about bestiality. It's a satirical attack on pigheaded rulers in an imaginary totalitarian state. As far as Hamlet. . . ."

"Borlinda, you're *new* at Horace Mann High, aren't you?"

"Yes," she said, visibly unhappy. "This will be my first semester here. For the past three years, I attended the Virgin Mary Bible Academy."

"You poor dear. How *relieved* you must be to escape that school."

"The fact is, Mr. Hamme. I miss my teachers there very much, and if my father hadn't died, if there were only enough insurance money, I would still be there for my last year."

"Well, Borlinda, I can't speak for your other teachers. But you can be certain in my class, I will expose you to new ways of thinking and new insights, which will shape your life forever."

"That's what I fear."

"You mustn't fear, Borlinda. You must enjoy. After all, life is like the *cannabis indica*. When properly cultivated, it will bring you pleasure beyond your wildest dreams."

"They always used to say at the Virgin Mary. . . ."

"Promise me something, Borlinda."

"What's that, Mr. Hamme?"

"Please don't mention that school again."

"Very well. But I was only going to say. . . ."

"Save it for our next talk. Now go to your class before you're late."

Virgin Mary Bible Academy! *My God, is that one going to be a challenge.* Hasn't the government learned yet the damage such schools are doing to our kids? They all ought to be *burned down* and replaced with schools like Horace Mann, schools committed to *creative* teaching. I must write my senator and *demand* student loans be denied to any private school that neglects to develop a student's creativity. I will emphasis in my letter that as long as Virgin Marys are permitted to produce *Polish* Borgias, our quality of life in America will continue to deteriorate.

Oh, what a wonderful world this would be if only we had more students like Mohammed Rajid. His paper for me on "Pregnancy Reduction Through Innovative Masturbation" was brilliant. That one idea, if ever disseminated, could drastically reduce unwanted pregnancies among the poor and disabled, saving the taxpayers millions of dollars in child support. But problem-solving students like Mohammed are rare. They require years of team teaching to produce. Without the support of the entire education establishment, students like him could easily be displaced by the Borgias. If that ever happens, I'll never be able to teach again in the public schools. After all, there's a limit to what one teacher—even a gifted teacher like me—can do in a classroom filled with Borgias.

It's so frustrating to have so much to give and no one to give it to. If only I had the *right* audience. Locked within me, *screaming* for release, are hundreds of years of wisdom, which I must dispense in bits and pieces. How long will I be able to hold back before I explode, splattering everywhere like the food crumbs left by the students? Oh, how difficult it is to stop teaching at the ringing of the last bell, especially after spending the day working myself up to a feverish pitch of brilliance. Though the students didn't always listen, though I sometimes had to use innovative teaching techniques, I still found it difficult to harness my energy and quit at three.

Oh, the suffering I must endure for being so brilliant.

To ease some of this suffering, I really ought to get involved in an after-school activity. But it can't be just *any* activity. It must be the *right* one, one that I can use to prepare the students intellectually for the day they will enroll in my lit class. Maybe an activity like the school paper, which would not only extend my teaching day, but would also become my forum for reaching *all* students—and even some of those *lazy* teachers. Yes, maybe running the school paper is the answer. Let's see if I can convince Pepe Noriega.

Pepe was sitting at his desk, writing, when I arrived. Even in repose, he revealed the fashionable air of a man who could change his image at the flip of a wrist. Dressed in a conservative blue suit, he looked like just another slim and attractive Latin male with prominent and mischievous brown eyes, until you lowered your gaze and saw his two fully developed female breasts. Then, another image immediately came to mind.

On his desk next to a small radio, which was beginning to play a samba, was a photograph of Tiny Tim, dancing gaily through the tulips while plucking his ukulele. It was signed: "To Pepita Love T.T." As I waited for him to finish writing, I found myself quietly yielding to my memories, which the music brought back, and my exciting summer South of the Border with fiery *señoritas*. Before I could disappear into my romantic past, touring Brazil's bordellos, Pepe switched stations, and I was quickly yanked back to the present with the harsh sounds of a Sousa march. Ignoring the music, I sat in a leather armchair and smoked one of his Cuban cigars that he kept on his desk for his men friends.

Thanks to his good taste in decorating I always felt welcome, visiting his office. The heavy oak desk, big leather armchairs, football trophies, and other masculine *objets d'art* made me feel at home. I often wondered why he didn't use a decorative style more suited to his personality, like French provincial furniture and crystal and silver curios. At such times, I believed he chose the men's club decor of leather and wood just to make sure that virile men like me always returned. For a buxom pansy, he certainly understood men.

Of course, I deserve some of the credit. As everyone knows, I have always been a strong influence in his life. Our friendship goes back many years, before he became known as Pepita and regarded by his classmates as "one of them." I met him during those happy years when he was the adored distant cousin to that super-macho Colombian who stuffed ballot boxes for a living. For Pepe, those were happy years with long vacations in Colombia and extravagant gifts from a doting male relative. But suddenly that all changed for him when he reached adolescence and his breasts developed. Almost immediately those gifts and trips ended, and his world collapsed. Even the boys at school abruptly rejected him—by taunting him with improper overtures!

As the strong, liberated male that I was, even in my youth, being his understanding friend then, was exactly what he needed to give him the strength to continue. Perhaps my greatest achievement, during those difficult years, was to introduce him to girls. At my insistence, we would double-date, and I would give him pointers on how to behave. Such a break from my studies, though difficult, was important because it provided me with the opportunity to teach a friend about girls. Sometimes, though, the lessons didn't turn out as planned, and our dates would get excited and start to fight over me. At such times, Pepe would have to keep the peace by sending me home alone.

Of course, I understood. I learned early in life that I was by far too irresistible. When girls were alone with me, they would become wild animals. It wasn't uncommon for them to scratch and bite and even kick during contact. That's why I made Pepe promise never to reveal my secret. The girls would probably kill for me if it ever became known about the monstrous size of my equipment (three inches when hard). In return, I promised never to tell anyone about his (six inches when soft). Of course, it would be pointless. The girls found it difficult to take me. Anything larger would be unmanageable.

How strange nature was. I mean being so generous to "one of them." It made no sense. He couldn't use it. Who could take it? Despite his abnormality, and maybe because of it, the boys unexpectedly took an interest in him. Although they no longer said nasty things to his face, I knew they still thought of him as a joke, one of those cosmic delights to be humored. It was only out of charity that Theta Omega (that all-jock fraternity) pledged him, and not me. It was much safer having him around. After all, he was nonthreatening and accommodating, and he didn't overwhelm them, as I did, with *awesome* virility.

While I filled my college years with my studies and swelled my brain with great literature, Pepe enjoyed himself as the Theta Omega amusement. In gratitude for my many years of masculine guidance, he personally saw to it that I was invited to the fraternity parties. Although as a nonmember I was never allowed inside the fraternity house, that never stopped me from attending. Pepe made certain

by leaving a chair outside. While I spent the evening in the
fresh air, watching the party fun through an open window,
Pepe would slip me beer and pizza. Although it would sometimes rain or snow, it still didn't dampen my enjoyment. I
always found it amusing to watch young men and women
behave with respectable restraint. None of that wild girl-
boy contact I knew when I was alone with women occurred.
For that reason, the parties would often end early, and the
party-goers would go upstairs in pairs to watch television
or talk. Sometimes, though, they would watch movies. That's
when someone would close the window and pull down the
shades. When I pressed my ear to the glass to listen, all I
could hear was a lot of heavy breathing. Since horror movies bored me, I would usually return to the dorm and study.

Yes, I was Pepe's loyal friend during those years. For
my loyalty, he made certain that the right people saw my
credentials and hired me, after I had lost my previous teaching job because of my revolutionary ideas on literature.

As the music finished playing the Sousa march, Pepe
put down his pen and began chatting.

"You know, Frank," he said. "You should've joined me
and Phyl Jaffe at the Club Saturday night. We had a *fabulous*
time—Phyl in her military surplus and me in my sequined
gown. Even Phyl who *never* touches boys (except, of course,
to fight) got turned on at the sight of me in drag. She just
loves it when I go braless, as do all the boys. Oh, the fun we
had—the dancing, the partying. Saturday nights just won't
be the same anymore without her. Damn, I'm going to miss
that woman."

"You two haven't broken up again, have you?"

"Didn't I tell you?" He paused, then added with a look
of melancholy, as though he were burying his best friend.
"She's gone straight!"

I sat bolt upright. "*Gone straight?*" I said. "You've got to
be kidding. That-hook-nose-bull-dyke-loan-shark's-daugh-

ter-from-Brooklyn is so crooked she doesn't know what straight is!"

"Please, Frank, you must learn to be a little more sensitive to differences. Remember, she *is* our superintendent, and next to you, my *dearest* friend!"

"I'm sorry, Pepe. I promise I'll be more politically correct in the future. But you've got to admit that's funny, in fact funnier than the time she told us she was related to the Jaffes of Britain. I mean, can you imagine, Phyl getting *serious* about a man."

"That isn't what she meant. What she meant is that she has found Christ and is giving up the ways of the world." His brown eyes settled on me, full of sadness, *full of purpose!* "Of course, this couldn't have happened to me at a worst time. Because of her decision, I no longer have an escort to the cotillion this weekend. Oh Frank, I just don't know *what* I'm going to do."

"Pepe," I said. "I know what you're thinking. But the answer is no!"

"Please Frank," he pleaded. "This is the *biggest* event of the year. *I've got to go!*"

"I can't, Pepe. I'll do anything for you. But not that. You know how women behave next to me. Can you imagine how horny fags (I mean gays) will behave if they ever got close to a real man? They'd never be able to control themselves."

"Don't you think you owe it to them to show them how a real man behaves in public? You could become their model, their. . . ."

"Please, Pepe," I interrupted. "I can't."

"It's better than doing nothing all weekend."

"You forget, Pepe, I've got my article to keep me busy."

"You're *still* working on that article?" he said, surprised. "It's been over two years!"

"Well, you must remember. I'm developing an original idea and developing an original idea is a slow process."

"But what can you possibly say that's new about Chaucer?"

"It's my belief, after reading the *Canterbury Tales* for the second time, that Chaucer was a transvestite sexist."

"*Transvestite sexist?*" he said, shocked.

"I'm sorry. Did I offend you?"

"Frank, you didn't offend me. You just surprised me. I just never thought Chaucer was one of the girls."

"Well, I still don't have all the facts. But I have come across some interesting research which indicates that maybe he was a little more flamboyant that history suggests, and just as soon as I have it all put together, I'll let you read it."

"You are such an original thinker, Frank. I look forward to reading anything you write."

"Thank you, Pepe. I am so pleased you recognize my talent."

"The important thing is, do the students?"

"I'm glad you brought that up. You know, Pepe, there's something seriously wrong with that senior class. There's just no fire in their soul. Why I haven't even seen one good fight since school started. And one of my students, a Virgin Mary dropout, had the effrontery to correct me. With students like that, how will I ever maintain standards?"

"Maybe education ought to become a cooperative effort, a democratic experience with the teacher and students as one."

"I don't think that's going to work. The only thing that works for them is when I display my manliness."

"How interesting," he said, and he began to run his hand lightly over his breast. For a moment, he revealed a look of pure ecstasy. I knew then he wasn't thinking about school, but about how sensational he was going to look braless in an evening dress. "Obviously what John Dewey once said must be true," he said. "'New problems demand for their intelligent solution the projection of new purposes, new ends in view; and new ends necessitate the development of new means and methods.' Of course, as we all know, new is not an absolute, and is only relative." He smiled. His mind seemed to be in the stratosphere, as his hand caressed his breast.

"Dewey is quite right, Pepe. But it really takes a great deal of energy to be new and effective when you have a classroom of students without imagination. Where did these kids come from? How did they *ever* complete three years of high school? Haven't their other teachers taught them *anything*?"

"Those are profound concerns, Frank, which we must leave to philosophers," he said, returning to earth. "What we must remember here at Horace Mann High is that the true center of a student's life isn't his school subjects, but instead his social activities."

Doesn't that fruit cake think of anything else?

"I agree with you one hundred percent, Pepe. In fact, the reason I so untiringly lecture my students is because I want them to become those well-adjusted social types you expect our graduates to be. Through my lessons, I hope to encourage them to grow and become fully realized men and women like you and me!"

"You're so dedicated, Frank," he said sincerely. "I'm sure a man with your vast knowledge will find all sorts of ways to reach your students."

"That's going to be a little difficult this term."

"Maybe there's an explanation for your failure. Maybe your students are just burned out from too much work. You know how greedy teenagers are. They're always lighting the candle at both ends. Sometimes all it takes to get their brain cells hopping again are some vitamins."

"What an excellent idea!" I said enthusiastically. "Why didn't I think of it? You know, Pepe. You really are quick. I guess that's why you're the principal, and I'm just a mere teacher. Sometimes I. . . ."

"What do you want, Frank?" he said suddenly.

"Want?" I said, acting confused.

"Come on, Frank. Get to the point. When you start flattering me, I know you are after something."

"Well, there is something I want to ask you."

"Which is?"

"It has to do with the school paper."

"I hope it isn't what I think it is. You know I promised the paper to Gullan this year."

"Can't you reconsider just this once?"

"That's impossible. That incisive article she published last year on the use of hallucinogenics to heighten the creative development among teenagers makes her qualifications for the job unassailable."

"You're absolutely right. In fact, I would be the last to deny it. But at moments like this, Pepe, you must be selfish. You must first think of yourself—and Saturday night's cotillion."

"Then you'll take me?"

"No, but I know who might."

"Who?"

"Niko Papalodopoulos."

"*Niko Papalodopoulos!*" he said, delighted. "Do you think he will? Do you honestly believe that magnificent Greek god will take me? Oh, if he did, I would truly be the belle of the ball." Pepe melted. "If you could pull that off, Frank, saying no to you for anything would be impossible."

"Then it's agreed?"

"Get me Niko, and you can have the paper!"

Two

With surprisingly good taste (at least, for a Greek), Niko transformed his broom-closet-size office, wedged between the gym and maintenance room, into a comfortable sanctuary. On the wall facing me were three floor-to-ceiling posters of the rocky and baron Delphic mountaintop where Apollo was worshipped. One poster was of the ruins of a theater, where Greek plays were performed; the other was of the temple of Apollo, where Pythia delivered her oracles in the adytun, and the third was of the gymnasium, where young athletes trained for the Pythian games. On the adjacent wall, framed simply in black, were the programs from the plays of Sophocles and Aristophanes. Above the programs, in a script, almost as elegant as mine, were the words "Know Thyself" (a sentiment, which I have so often imparted to my students).

Beneath the programs were two Doric columns of different sizes. On top of the shortest, there was a statue of Apollo playing with himself (or was it a cithara?); and on top of the tallest, there was the head of some Greek thinker who had lost his nose, sticking it in the wrong place. Next to the columns was Niko, a dark-haired man with a vigorous body, broad chest and slim hips.

Dressed like an ordinary working-class man in khakis, white shirt and tie, he was sitting on a stone bench, reading a book with the intellectual air of a Mongoloid sage. Some might think, if they liked the masculine Mediterranean type, that he was handsome, and in a Neanderthal way, he might be to demented queens like Pepita. As far as I was concerned, he had too much nose and lips, and he lacked the refinement of Good English Stock. After all, he was a Greek and the son of an immigrant cook, and his only good fortune was having enough wit to win a scholarship to college, where he managed to persuade the faculty to graduate him *summa cum laude.*

My first thought was to sit next to him and, while gazing at the posters, quietly yield to the serenity of that beautiful Delphic mountaintop where the spirit of Apollo resided. But I wisely resisted the temptation, and stood instead. The seat was just a little too low to be suitable for someone as tall and elegant as I.

Despite my disapproval of Niko, I had to admit he was a clever counselor who understood the basic needs of man. His schooling had successfully prepared him for counseling by training him to recognize that one of man's basic needs was to escape city madness and commune with the gods.

As I have often told my seniors, the real purpose of education is to introduce us to Eternal Truth. Where else, but at Delphi, could Truth be so eloquently revealed. Those magnificent ruins, surrounded by an azure sky on that sensuous mountiantop, were the perfect setting for a spiritual awakening. Just gazing at the posters made me yearn to be there where I could be one with the gods. Perhaps by remaining dedicated to teaching Truth, this wish will be granted. Who knows? For my dedication, I might be rewarded by being reincarnated as a tree or a stream or a snow-capped mountain. Could I be so brazen to hope? But why shouldn't I? Why shouldn't this be my reward for *nobly* teaching?

As I gazed at the posters, I found myself slipping back in time. Images of Apollo (or, as we English prefer to call him, that primitive apple-tree god) immediately came to mind. While observing the temple where Pythia had delivered the oracles, I remembered a scene from that cinematic classic I had seen at the adult bookstore about the secret love of Apollo. In that scene, the woman who played Pythia was lying at the altar of Delphi where she and Apollo made music and poetry together. The sheer beauty of their union came back with a rush and filled me with excitement.

While standing there, remembering, the room slowly grew dark. Above me I saw the galaxy, and in the background, hidden in the ruins, someone began to play a bouzouki. Illuminated by a heavenly light, Pythia and Apollo began moving together in time to the pagan, lusty sounds of the music. Seeing them entwined made me yearn to be with them. Before I could rush to the temple and join the happy couple, I was halted by a voice.

The voice was gentle and angelic. It surrounded me as though I were in the center of it. "Thank you, Frank, for coming," the voice said, "You can't imagine how long I've waited for this moment, how thrilled I am that you have finally come."

I turned in hope of glimpsing the form that complemented the voice, but I saw nothing except darkness and the galaxy above.

As I stared into the galaxy, into the Great Beyond, I noticed one star had unexpectedly grown brighter than the others, and it was twinkling. *Twinkling at me!*

"Talk to me, Frank," the voice coaxed. "Tell me what's on your mind so I can lead you to the light."

"There's so much to tell," I said excitedly, staring intently at the twinkling star. "I don't know where to begin."

"Begin anywhere, Frank. Just let it out. Tell me *everything!*"

"Well, I could begin with that senior class," I said to the star.

"Then begin there, Frank, and tell me all!"

"Well, today I poured out my soul again, filled the classroom with the wisdom of the ages—and nothing happened. *Nothing happened!* What's wrong with those kids? What could've possibly been done to their minds to close them so firmly to new ideas?"

"Frank, it's not them," the omnipresent voice said. "It's you. When are you going to wise up and face the facts?"

"Me?! Frank Hamme! *You've got to be crazy!* I'll have you know, my noble ancestry goes back to the time of the Suscrofas. In fact, it was a Suscrofa who made history killing the first wild boar for food, then serving it to the ancient Celts. So it can't be me. It's obviously *them!* I'm an Englishman with a distinguished lineage, born to serve the food of life to the bards."

"Oh, why don't you shut up, and quit teaching!"

"Quit teaching?" I said, startled. *"Never!"* I was firm, ready to fight the Olympian gods themselves, to defend my calling. "Frank Hamme is first and foremost a teacher. I shall never be anything less. *NEVER!"*

The lights went on, and the office once again became a room with posters and an allusion to Delphi. "You're an idiot," Niko said. "Now tell me what's really on your mind!" I turned to him, and saw a microphone and a small control panel on the floor next to the bench.

How clever he is. That man almost had me. He almost broke me down and got me to confess. How could I have been so vulnerable? I had been warned of his revolutionary approach to counseling by my students. They told me how quickly he established contact and how easily he cut to the core. So there's no excuse for my behavior. None whatsoever. Yet I didn't protect myself. I walked into his office with my guard down and fell right into his trap.

Imagine, if I could succumb (me, Frank Hamme, with my superior knowledge), how overwhelming he must be for the students. In just a few moments, he could destroy hundreds of years of education, reverse mankind, throw us back into the dark ages. All because he wants us to submit to the most depraved and unnatural act known to man— *thinking!*

Oh, what a hateful, dangerous man he is.

Niko was smiling, amused by my vulnerability, as though aware of what was running through my mind. I felt an urge to use that statue of Apollo playing with himself to change the size and shape of Niko's nose, but decided against it.

"That's quite a technique you've got," I said, then added scornfully, "Nick!"

"The name's Niko, Mr. Hamme with the silent 'E'. And I must admit the students like it too. It's amazing how much I learn about what's going on here when I use it."

"You have no shame," I said. I then locked gazes with him, determined to make him feel guilty for his treasonable behavior. "Thank god I've done a little checking on you, and I know what you're up to."

"Tell me, Frank," he said, more amused than interested. "What am I up to?"

"Don't play innocent with me," I said scornfully. "I know all about your plans to overthrow the public schools of America. Well, you're not going to get away with it. I won't let you!"

He surprised me by laughing. It was a deep manly laugh, which intensified my anger. "You're hilarious, Frank. You must keep those kids rolling in the aisles."

"Don't you take that attitude with me! You. . .you *subversive*. Hasn't it ever occurred to you the irreparable damage you're doing to kids by teaching them to think, instead of going with the flow? If what you're doing was ever made public, every government agency in America would come after you. Even Pepe would have to throw you and your little show out on its ass."

"Save it, Frank. You didn't come here to flex your muscle," he said, no longer amused. "Get to the point. What do you want?"

I almost forgot the real purpose of my visit by allowing my anger to take charge. I mustn't do that. I mustn't allow anything to interrupt my mission. Later, when I'm in a better position. Then I'll take that Minoan bull by the horns and really do some acrobats on him! In the meantime, I'll just have to measure my words, and be pleasant.

"Well, Frank, speak up!"

I hesitated. I didn't know how to word it. After all, how does a man ask another man to take a fruit cake to a dance? Oh why does that queen always put me in these awkward situations?

"Frank," he said impatiently. "I don't have all day."

"I don't know where to begin," I said, embarrassed.

"Anywhere. Just get to the point."

"Very well," I blurted out. "Can you take Pepe to the cotillion Saturday night?"

"Is that all?"

"Well, yes, of course."

"Then tell Pepe, yes. I've never been to one of those fag balls, and. . . ."

"I think it would be better if you referred to it as a cotillion. You might offend Pepe by calling it a fag ball."

"Very well, you can tell Pepe that I would be delighted to take him to the cotillion, under one condition."

"What's that?"

"He keeps his hands on his lap!"

"Agreed," I said. "I'll tell Pepe to keep his hands on his lap. But you must ask him to go yourself. It would finalize the arrangement."

"Very well. Anything else?"

"Nothing that I can think of."

"Then good-bye." He picked up his book and began to read.

I became very suspicious of Niko's quickness to agree. Clever men like Niko who spend their lives manipulating people don't agree so quickly without a reason. I better keep an eye on him. He may be up to something.

I was collecting my mail, when I saw Pepe's breasts peek from his office. I didn't need to ask what was on his mind. I knew the moment he stepped into the outer office and greeted me.

"Frank," he called. There was an urgency in his voice, almost desperation. "Can I see you please?"

"Of course." I casually read the announcement of the faculty meeting, sorted through a few letters, studied the promotion from a book club, then entered his office leisurely. "I see we're having a faculty meeting tomorrow. What's the subject?"

"Nothing important," he said, closing the door behind me. "Something about drug awareness week. Now tell me, Frank. Did you ask him?"

"Who?"

"Frank, don't play with me. You know perfectly well whom I'm talking about."

"Oh you mean, the Greek stud?"

"That's right," he said, obviously not in the mood for delays. "What did he say?"

I looked at him, and didn't reply. I wanted to tease him with silence. When I was certain he couldn't take the delay any longer, when I was absolutely positive he was ready to leap on me and physically force me to respond, I said simply, "He said yes."

"He said yes?" he repeated, surprised.

"That's right, Pepe. He said yes."

Pepe was suddenly Pepita. He was on his toes, whirling around, dancing. I haven't seen him like this since he was pledged to that all-jock fraternity in college. "Oh Frank, how can I thank you? How can I ever show my appreciation?"

I smiled. This was the moment I was waiting for, and I was determined to take full advantage of it. "Well, now that I'm going to be running the school paper, you can start by giving me a computer."

"You'll get it. You'll get it," he said. And he was still in motion, moving around the room like a prima ballerina. "He said yes. *Niko Papalodopoulos said yes.* Oh, Frank, isn't that wonderful? Why I'll be the envy of the ball. Me, Pepita Noriega will be attending the ball with a *genuine* man. How exciting!" He stopped all motion, and suddenly became quite concerned. "Oh Frank, I just had a *horrible* thought. What will I wear? You must help me select something. Say you will, Frank. Please. I *desperately* need a man's point of view."

"Of course, I'll help you. Now about the computer. As you know, a computer is worthless without a printer."

"Okay, okay. I'll get you a printer. . . ."

"But it must be laser."

"Very well, laser. I'll use some of the money reserved for books to buy you one. How about coming over after school? You can have dinner at my place, and we can review my wardrobe for ideas."

"I can't today."

His dark brown eyes suddenly burst into flame. "*What do you mean you can't today?!*" Pepita was now Pepe, the tough, on-my-terms-only, hot-tempered-Latin administrator.

"I scheduled an after-school activity."

"*Cancel it!*"

"But I'll disappoint the students."

"Frank," his voice was dangerous.

"All right. I'll make the meeting short. But under one condition. . . ."

He looked at me suspiciously. "What's it this time?"

"A computer and a laser printer to be useful need the right software and fonts. So Pepe, is it possible. . . ."

He arched one of his well-plucked eyebrows. "Frank, are you trying to take advantage of my kindness?"

"Of course not, Pepe." I said. "I just want to turn out the best paper I can. That's all."

"Well, don't," he said. "You know how the Board is. The more professional you are, the less support you get."

"I know. Still, the right software can make a difference between a salable and unsalable newspaper."

"Very well. I'll see what I can do about pirating you a word processing program and some fonts. But that's got to be it, Frank. That's absolutely the *maximum* I can do for you at this time. Now about dinner. Is six all right?"

"That's fine."

"Oh I can't wait." And Pepe once again became Pepita, all motion, all girl. "We'll have such fun tonight. I just love dressing up for a man."

"Incidentally," I said, "it's only fair to warn you. Niko has put a condition on the date."

"He has put a condition on our first date!?" Pepe said, shocked.

"He wants you to promise to keep your hands on your lap."

"How will we ever dance if I must keep my hands on my lap?"

"Who touches these days? Everyone just sort of moves by themselves to the music."

"In case you've forgotten, Frank, this is a cotillion, not a disco dance."

"Well, that's what he told me. But I am certain, once he sees how gorgeous you look all dressed up, all his inhibitions will break down. I have great faith in Pepita. When she mambos, all the boys say cha-cha-cha."

"Please, Frank," he corrected me. "You know I don't mambo."

"There's only one way to run a newspaper. As Joseph Pulitzer once said, 'What a newspaper needs in its news, in its headlines, and on its editorial page is accuracy, accuracy, accuracy!' Those words must become our words. They must appear on the masthead, and echo in every printed word. The readers of *The Inquisitor* must believe unquestionably what we publish has been checked and rechecked and what we say is accurate, accurate, *accurate!*"

That's what I said to the seven students who arrived. That was the theme of my talk to those pimple-faced, gum-chewing, burned-out, slang-ridden idiots whom through the magic of teaching I was going to turn single-handedly into Pulitzer-Prize-winning journalists.

The eighth whom I deliberately didn't count was that impenetrable mass of protoplasm, that nightmare from my sixth-period English class, that Virgin Mary Bible Academy dropout, *Borlinda Borgia!* True to her type, she sat in the front row like a saint, legs pressed together, hands clasped, as though waiting to be blessed by the pope himself.

As I expounded on journalism, as I filled the small room with my heavenly baritone voice, I became uncomfortably aware of the way she was studying *me*, not my manhood, but *me*, with that look of a vestal virgin, chosen to keep an eye on the sacred fire burning on her altar!

"Never forget," I said, "journalists are *noble* professionals, who, like teachers, must dedicate themselves to Truth. Here at *The Inquisitor*, it won't be any different. Our freedom of speech, which the Constitution so carefully protects in the Fifth Amendment. . . ."

"First Amendment, Mr. Hamme," the Virgin Mary dropout corrected politely. "The Fifth Amendment safeguards accused persons, and the First Amendment. . . ."

"Thank you, Borlinda."

"You're welcome, Mr. Hamme," she said politely. I glanced at her, annoyed, then resumed with my talk.

After I had dazzled them for an hour with my enormous knowledge of the intimate and sometimes naughty behavior of great journalists, I told them about Jonathan Wright and recounted in detail some of his flamboyant escapades (including those I couldn't remember) that shocked America. I hoped by his example to give them an idea of what a good journalist ought to be, the type of person they should all try to emulate.

"Unlike other publishers of his day, Jonathan courageously concentrated on the big three—sex, drugs and murder," I summed up. "By doing this, he had successfully freed Americans of their middle-class innocence, and opened their eyes to the real world where negotiating was done, not in board rooms, but in dark alleys. His dedication to the realities of life, his passion for digging for Truth (no matter where it took him) was what made him great. This type of greatness is what I look for in a journalist. So with that in mind, tell me briefly about yourself. Tell me why you think you would be a good journalist. Let's start with you, Bea."

"My mama used to always say, 'Bea,' she'd say, 'You gonna be a great newspaper woman 'cause there ain't nobody who can gossip like you.'"

"I don't know much about writing," another student said. "But I sure can take good pictures in dark bedrooms."

"You want truth. Ask me, Jeremiah Brown. No one can keep a secret from me. I know exactly how to squeeze it from them."

"Oh, my," I said, impressed. "You all sound so professional."

While the others were telling me about themselves, my gaze settled on Roger Murphy, an athletic-looking student in tight, torn Levi's and a T-shirt with "Say Yes to Vitamins" on it. He reminded me of someone who spent his spare time lifting weights and shopping in health stores. When he saw me stare, he casually smiled and spread his legs. He was obviously trying to let me know, in his subtle way, that I wasn't the only man in the room. I noticed that Borlinda Borgia also noticed him. Although he was sitting behind her, she still managed to observe him without being obvious. Several times under the pretense of straightening her blonde hair, she would use her hand mirror to catch glimpses of him. I smiled, pleased.

There's hope for that girl after all.

After assigning everyone a responsibility, based on their special talents, I turned my attention to Borlinda. "Now Bor, why don't you tell us about your journalism experience?"

"Certainly, Mr. Hamme," she said politely. "First of all, I am a perfect speller, and I have an excellent grasp of language, and for two years, I was the star reporter for the *Virgin Mary Bible Beacon*. . . ."

"*The Virgin Mary Bible Beacon?*" I asked curiously.

"That was our school paper," she said proudly. "It won all kinds of awards from the Coalition of Private Schools for the Advancement of Christian Education. Now as far as my professional experience, last summer I worked with. . . ."

"Very impressive, Borlinda. Language skills are important, no doubt. But they aren't sufficient for a journalist. Pick up any publication, and you'll find that it's not language skill that makes journalists great (though they do have a certain sensitivity to the vernacular), but it's their ability to recreate reality. A good journalist takes you into the gutter where he lets you wallow *sympathetically* in the slime! That, Borlinda, is the mark of a first-class reporter. That, Borlinda, is the type of person I need on the beat, digging up the news. You, though, well, you Borlinda. . . ."

And I began to think about my grand plan for her. Until I fully realized it (and had the opportunity to implement it),

I couldn't possibly let her become a reporter. With her eye for detail, she would probably come back with the wrong story.

After all, how could she relate to truth, when all she knew were those holy tales taught to her at that Bible factory? How could she understand heads, pimps, and sluts when she was preoccupied with right and wrong? How could she achieve Nirvana, when her body had never been emancipated? I had to free her somehow, send her soaring.

But that's not going to be easy. She's living reason why it's urgent (and I must include this in my letter to the senator) that the government takes complete control of *all* education from infancy to adulthood. By removing kids from their home before parents can misguide them, professionals like me will be in a better position to successfully shape them into adults appropriate for *civilized* society!

But what about the Borlinda Borgias? What do I do with them in the meantime?

"You, Borlinda," I said, after considerable thought, "You belong here with me. Your eye for detail, your propensity for accuracy is exactly what we need at the copy desk. You will be the perfect person to edit all the material these talented journalists bring to us to publish. You will be my proofreader and assistant editor. I can be certain with your sensitivity to language you will remove the excess and reduce each story to its essence (to the simple and the direct) which will be the hallmark of *The Inquisitor*. Who knows? Maybe because of your skills our humble newspaper may someday win awards too?"

I was pleased to notice that she beamed with delight. Developing the Angel of God's potential won't be difficult after all. In my skilled hands, it should be quite routine.

After I dismissed them, everyone left except Roger. He lingered, and closed the door.

"Do you mind if we talk?" Roger asked.

"By all means. I welcome the opportunity to talk to students and share with them my knowledge. After all, something I might say to them might be of special importance at a time when they most need it."

"I like that attitude. You're really quite a hunk. . .I mean, teacher."

"I would like to think I'm also quite a hunk."

"You are," he smiled. "But I'm sure you've been told that before."

"Yes, I have. Many times. Now tell me. What did you most appreciate about what I had to say?"

"That's a tough one, Mr. Hamme. You say so many brilliant things. Take for example what you said in class several days ago about Hamlet. Now that was really deep!"

"Why thank you, Roger," I said. "You can't imagine how pleased I am to realize that I *am* appreciated by the class, and that I haven't just been casting my pearls to swine."

"I can't speak for the others. Only for myself," he said. "But as far as I was concerned, you were brilliant."

"Oh, I'm so glad you think so. But it worries me, and it has worried me for some time. How can I get my message across to the other seniors? They don't seem to have your sensitivity to great ideas. In fact, they seem quite *in*sensitive."

"That's because they need some of my vitamins to perk them up."

"You sell vitamins?"

"I sure do," he said proudly. "It's a little business I've just started with a Colombian friend."

"You know, it's interesting that you mention vitamins. I was talking to the principal earlier, and he said the same thing."

"He's right. A few vitamins are all any of us need. That, and an occasional smoke." He then offered me a small, hand-rolled cigarette.

"Is this the aromatic brand you are always smoking after class?"

He smiled. "That's right. It's my own special blend of natural herbs."

"Herbs?" I said, impressed. "Amazing."

"I learned all about it in a science class from a sub we had a few weeks ago."

He lighted the cigarette for me. When I blew the smoke out, he objected. "You're supposed to inhale deeply and swallow the smoke." He took the cigarette and demonstrated.

I tried again. This time I swallowed the smoke, as he suggested. I found myself immediately soaring. "This cigarette is *wonnn-der-ful*," I said, grabbing a chair for support. "You must tell me that sub's name so we can get him back right away."

"You think the cigarette's good. You should try my vitamins."

"You know what?"

"What, Mr. Hamme."

"Call me Frank."

"Very well. What, Frank?"

"If your vitamins are as good as these cigarettes, why don't you sell them to the seniors before class. A simple pill may be all they need to get their brain cells hopping again!"

"That's a great idea, Frank."

"Of course," I added sensibly, "as your teacher and mentor—for allowing you to use the classroom for your little business venture—I should be entitled to a cut. Say about $50 a week?"

"That's a lot, Frank. My costs are too high for that kind of split. How about $10 instead?"

"Of course, I'm sure you know that Pepe would never approve of your business activity during school hours, but I could easily turn my back and say nothing for about—well, maybe $20 a week."

"That's pretty stiff, Frank. I'm still just the new guy on the block, and I have huge start-up costs. Let's make it $15. That's really the best I can do at this time."

"All right, but under one condition."

"What's that?"

"You throw in a few cigarettes occasionally."

"Deal."

Three

The teachers weren't concerned that Pepe was already ten minutes late for the morning faculty meeting. Accustomed to his tardiness, they simply napped or gossiped instead of complain. I, on the other hand, used the time wisely and pondered great thoughts!

When Pepe finally arrived, all of the teachers sprung to attention. Those who were napping were awakened by friends. No one wanted to miss Pepe's grand entrance. There was something wonderfully whimsical about seeing him—or rather his two huge breasts—in motion. It was like watching a braless woman with a man's head in men's clothing vigorously exercise. As often as we had seen it, we still wanted to see more.

"I'm so sorry I'm late," he said, pressing his hand against his breasts to still them (or was he massaging them?) "I was tied up in an important conference with the counselor and lost all track of time. So I promise I'll be brief. I know how firm the union contract is about the number and length of faculty meetings, and I am the first to yield to its directives. But I felt we needed to talk today, and I was sure you wouldn't mind my taking liberties with your before-class time just this once."

I sensed by the pointless chatter that he was in a talkative mood. Just the thought of him filling the room with words made me restless to leave and have one of those wonderful herbal cigarettes Roger blended.

"Yesterday I lunched with Phyl Jaffe," he said. "For those new to the area, Phyl is that sexy, mannish superintendent who is always being photographed by the press wearing those cute pants suits and adorable Salvador-Dalí-designed ties. Anyway, while Phyl and I were sharing a smoke in the alley near the Harlequin Room, she says in the strictest of confidence. 'Pepe,' she says, 'you tell your teachers to avoid *La Esperanza!* The owner (one of those Colombian refuges) went and got himself into trouble with the government for tax evasion or something, and there may be a raid.' So for those of you needing medication or foreign cigarettes, she recommends you head over to the Half-Moon House. It's owned by a very macho Afro-American called Kelly. Incidentally, Kelly also runs a travel agency, and he is offering a special ten-day educational tour this Christmas to the Golden Triangle, which should be lots of fun for those of you interested in growing your own poppies. I don't know exactly where the Half-Moon House is, but I understand it's near Seventh and Market. Please remember that the only reason I'm telling you this about *La Esperanza* is because I don't want you caught in any raid or scandal that may embarrass the good name of our school."

"Should we warn our students about *La Esperanza?*" one teacher asked.

"I'm glad you brought that up. I think Frank should do that in the next issue of the school paper. For those of you who haven't heard, he will be our new editor of *The Inquisitor.* Finally, don't forget. Next month we are going to celebrate Drug Awareness Week. The President—who will start campaigning for reelection soon—is quite interested in what we do in the schools. As you know, these past few years have been especially embarrassing for him—thanks to double-digit inflation, government scandal, rioting, and that absurd paternity suit by his former live-in housekeeper, Fifi LaRue. To divert attention from such negative publicity during the upcoming election year, he is anxiously trying to get the public focused on important social issues. For this he needs our help. So let's help the man who is giving us bigger and more expensive schools. Let's incorporate the dangers of drugs into our lessons for D.A. Week and support the President's dream of keeping drugs out of the home by getting kids to *squeal* on their parents!" He glanced about the room. "Any other questions?"

"I have one," a teacher said. "How will we recognize this Kelly?"

"Believe me. You'll have no trouble. He's a *divine*-looking six-foot-five black man with a half-moon scar across his left cheek. You'll see him from time to time on Market Street, wearing colorful clothes. You know, green pants, red shirt, white shoes. That sort of thing. However, a word of caution. He hangs out with some tough Jamaicans, and I understand he can be mean. There are some ugly stories about how he got that scar. So be nice to him and pay your bills promptly, and you should have no trouble. From what Phyl tells me, because his little store is new, his prices will be quite competitive. Many political types frequent his place, *including* the mayor."

Many faculty members, thrilled about this inside information, expressed eagerness to visit the Half-Moon House during their lunch break.

I was about to leave with the other teachers when Pepe stopped me and began to talk about the weather. After wearing me out, exhibiting his endless collection of ball gowns last night, I knew the weather wasn't what was on his mind.

"Frank," he said excitedly, after the last teacher had left. "He stopped by. Niko Papalodopoulos stopped by this morning and asked me to the cotillion." He began to dance like Ginger Rogers with an imaginary Fred Astaire, lots of spins and graceful dips. "You know what that big Greek stud said?" He stopped all motion and looked me in the eye. "He said it would be all right if I touched him while dancing. Oh, how he teases me. That adorable man has *no* shame. Well, that's all right. Let him. I'm still the luckiest girl in the world. I'm going to the cotillion with a *man!*"

"Well, just watch yourself," I said cautiously. "He's supposed to be a very *clever* man."

"Oh, I *love* clever men!"

"I don't mean that way. So just be careful what you say and do."

"I make no promises when I am out with a man."

"Well, I've warned you. Now you'll have to excuse me. I've got a class to teach."

Seeing a friend lose control of himself over such a man disturbed me. Why couldn't he be more like me—a little stronger? I just don't understand his attraction to Niko. But more important, that Greek's attraction to that hermaphrodite. Is it possible I may be wrong about Niko, that beneath his masculine facade is another queen? If that's the case, I have nothing to worry about. But if it isn't, if Niko is out to use Pepe, I have a great deal to worry about. After all, Niko is a skilled counselor, and he does have a reputation for wanting to overthrow the public schools!

Yes, I better keep an eye on him. I can't allow some Greek of questionable ancestry to use my dear friend shamelessly to advance his corrupt dream. It could interfere with *my* plans for the school.

True, I am a *little* older than my students (light-years intellectually), yet they still think of me as smashingly handsome and desirable (thanks to Elizabeth Arden and plastic surgery). Part of my ageless appeal is my ability to appear wiser and older (but *never* old). Conveying this image has been remarkably easy. I do it simply by wearing the right clothes and by maintaining the right youthful attitude.

Today, for example, feeling savagely sexy, I wear an Italian cut shirt, unbuttoned just enough to reveal my 18-carat-gold-chain necklace and my hairy chest. Revealing both the necklace and the hairy chest is very important. The necklace conveys personal commitment, which quietly informs the girls that they may look, but they can't touch, and the hairy chest, I've learned a long time ago, gives me that irresistible Italian look. Girls (and certain types of boys) like my fuzzy chest, particularly when I darken the fair hair with dye and the creamy white skin with sunlight. It suggests virility and youthfulness (which I have in abundance). But most important, it announces to the world that there is a man under those form-fitting clothes who takes life seriously. Nothing appeals to precocious teenagers more than to see a handsome, virile man strut his stuff, which I proudly do five hours a day, Monday through Friday, and for one additional hour Tuesday and Thursday while working on the school newspaper. Even I get excited at the sight of me in motion.

Teaching, though, isn't all show and glitter. No one knows that more than I. As a teacher (and humanitarian), I'm faced daily with the responsibility of encouraging my students to free themselves. Only by getting them to release their primal needs for the entire world to enjoy can I successfully fulfill my societal obligation of *noblesse oblige!*

But what really makes me proud to be a teacher (and is probably my greatest service to mankind) is what occurs on a more subtle level. By encouraging them to release themselves freely, I am in a position to influence them and to shape their dreams so that they are in harmony with Nature. I do this by quietly planting ideas in their heads, which will grow and merge with other ideas to become important *new* ideas. Who knows when and how this will occur. It could be years

from now while reading a newspaper article, or talking to a
friend or while undergoing a personal tragedy (like vasec-
tomy). But suddenly it happens. All the information I so
diligently gave them begins to make sense. At that moment
a truly special person is born, like a Tom Wong who psycho-
analyzed John Stuart Mill or a Igor Ivanovich who reinter-
preted *Hamlet*.

Such successes make me feel like a sculptor, a
Michelangelo, capable of shaping granite into something
beautiful. At least that's how Wong and Ivanovich made me
feel. With these seniors, though, it's another matter.

Here I am entrusted with the brightest and the best students in the city, the *cream* of America's teenagers, and none
of my gems flung to them are gathered—except during those
special moments when I show my manly stuff. It makes me
wonder what happened to them? Maybe it is true what I
had once heard, maybe there is a conservative backlash,
which is changing America, and this is the result, this is the
future which we, as educators, must face.

As I waited for Roger to finish selling his pills, I hoped
he and Pepe were right about the vitamins. If they were, it
could change the direction of history. Judging from Roger's
brisk classroom business, it shouldn't take long before I
started to see results.

"Henry Miller, class," I said, after Roger had given me
the signal to begin, "once made an important and wise
observation. This great twentieth century writer said that
obscenity in literature and poetry existed, not for excitation,
but for a purpose *beyond* sex. To confirm this, all we need to
do is examine any good piece of writing, and we will discover
profundities that will exceed our expectations. The poems
of Gaius Valerius Catullus will do for an example. As many
times as I have read this refreshing Greek poet. . . ."

"Mr. Hamme," a voice said suddenly. "Catullus isn't a
Greek name. It's Italian."

I glanced at Borlinda, the Italian nun responsible for that observation. "Thank you, Borlinda," I said politely, allowing my smile to conceal my annoyance. "Now as I was saying, in really *good* poetry and literature, we must learn to penetrate the surface for the hidden meaning. Keeping that in mind, how would you interpret this poem?

'A man who sees a pretty boy
Walking with a salesman.
What should he think but that the boy
Was looking for a buyer?'"

I awaited a response. There was silence. "Let me repeat the poem," I then reread it. I again waited for a response. More silence.

Finally, when I was about to read it for the third time, someone blurted out: "It sounds to me like it's about a pimp and a male whore."

"Wrong," I said. "On the surface, that may *seem* true, but that isn't what Catullus *actually* had in mind. The message he wanted to convey is more metaphysical. Let's examine it carefully by translating some of the key words." I read the poem again. "First of all, the main image that leaps from the pages is of a man and a boy. The careful reader immediately makes the association of the older and the wiser leading the younger and the more innocent to their intellectual salvation. The adjective pretty is placed before boy to convey the high metaphysical value he has to the intellectual scheme of life. Translated, this means his intellectual salvation is the ultimate purpose of existence, which is why the word salesman is used to identify the man. The man is a salesman of philosophy, very much as I'm a salesman of literature, and the boy who's with him isn't looking for a buyer in any mundane sense. Instead, he's looking for Eternal Truth, which this salesman of philosophy can lead him to."

The class just listened with their mouths open. What could they say? After all, I had just opened the heavenly gates of wisdom for them by condensing eloquently the hidden meaning of a great poem?

"Now this is how you should read poetry and literature. You must always look *beyond* the surface to the *true* meaning! To hasten your understanding, I am going to introduce you to some of the most thrilling works of literature available. I will include such eminent and capable writers as Jean Genet, Henry Miller, Norman Mailer, and of course Catullus. My purpose is to uncover their real themes, the profundities beyond the lust and sex (that modestly exists in some of their writings), and identify the truths hidden by metaphors, waiting for you to discover."

A hand began to wave in the air. It was the familiar hairless hand of the virtuous Miss Borgia. I could tell by the way her blue eyes lighted up that she was agitated by something I had said, and I suspected any moment she was going to make a statement that would challenge my position. My first reaction was to ignore her and continue with my lecture. But I knew that wouldn't be wise. The class enjoyed our meeting of the minds, and I noticed, whenever she spoke, all the students would sit up and listen. Therefore, it was my responsibility to respond to her questions and to convince the class once again what a knowledgeable man I was— *by quickly putting the little upstart in her place!*

"Yes, Borlinda," I said sweetly.

"I'm confused. Last time you told us to search for the love angle. And now you're telling us to search for a deeper metaphysical truth. What should we look for, Mr. Hamme, the love angle or the metaphysical truth?"

That girl infuriates me. She takes everything I say so literally. How can I be spontaneous? How can I be me, if she insists on measuring each word I utter and continuously steps between me and free thought?

"That great metaphysical truth which I speak of, which all poets and writers speak of, is very simply love, Miss

Borgia. Until you experience it yourself, you can not grasp its profound significance and understand how it can unite us all in one orgastic union."

"If that's true, Mr. Hamme, then how can you say that obscenity in literature is for a larger purpose beyond lust and sex when you define that metaphysical end to be carnal in nature?"

A big smile spread across the class. Almost immediately, the students jabbed each other with elbows, slapped palms, and one boy even brazenly laughed. "Listen to that girl go," he said. "She sure is *hot* today."

When the excitement had passed, and I had everyone's full attention, I said in my most academic voice: "Miss Borgia, when I use the word love, it's only as a metaphor for a concept *beyond* the carnal. I suggest you read Plato's *Meno* or that interesting modern update, *Jim Jones in Guyana* for a clarification of my position. Now class, as I was saying. . . ."

I noticed the moment I took control of the lecture again and put Borlinda in her place all interest in what I had to say ceased. For the majority, the only thing that awakened them from their mental slumber were those brief interactions with that demented Polish ex-patriot.

Roger Murphy was the exception. Stretched out in the back of the room, his feet on the desk, his chair precariously tilted, he listened intently to everything I said. For fifty minutes, I became the light leading him to Valhalla, a Socrates shaping his mind to match the splendor of his body.

By the way the girls worshipped him (some brazenly) and the boys obeyed him (some fearfully), I knew Roger was what I needed as an example for the others. Who knows what I might create with a little patience? Maybe because of my influence, he might someday become another Hamme.

Oh, how lucky he is to have someone like me to guide him.

While pondering his good fortune, my gaze drifted to the wall, where I had hung my degrees, and settled affectionately on my coat of arms. Immediately I gasped. During my years of teaching, I have tolerated boredom, indifference, even ignorance. *But nothing like this!*

If ever I find out who did this, if ever I catch the mental misfit responsible, I will ram his ass with the tusks of my ancestral boar. I will pierce his thick hide with a Suscrofa poison arrow. And if that's not enough, I will trample what's left of his balls with the mighty weight of the family armor.

HOW DARE THAT LITTLE PRICK TURN UPSIDE DOWN MY COAT OF ARMS!

The editorial meeting was a disaster. None of the students had any fresh ideas for the first issue of *The Inquisitor*. What ideas they did have were unoriginal and dull, and at best fragments of thought. Somehow I had to provide them with a suitable lead, but with this group that wasn't going to be easy, since none of them revealed the type of imagination needed to take an idea into flight. It's a pity their other teachers weren't doing their job as conscientiously as I. Maybe then my work wouldn't be so difficult.

"Let's try again," I said to the staff. "Remember, you are journalists who want to be read. So let's come up with interesting and *original* ideas."

"How about an article on the counselor," one boy said. "I hear that Greek has some real way-out ideas about education."

Oh dear, Niko's the last person I want to attack, not as long as Pepe feels the way he does about him. No, that story will never work, at least not now.

"First, you must never call him a Greek," I said to the boy. "That's too derogatory. As newspaper men and women, you must be sensitive to words. So please remember that in the future. Now regarding Mr. Papalodopoulos," I continued, "he is a very professional counselor. True, he does have some unorthodox ideas about education. But you must learn to forgive him for that. Remember, someday you may need him, and when that day comes, it'll be nice to know that he's there for you." I smiled, hoping I had squelched that idea. "Again, back to my question, what suggestions are there for a lead story?"

"We could do a piece on the principal's tits."

There was general laughter.

"We must be serious. You know if we ever mentioned her (excuse me, I mean *him*) except with the kindest and most affectionate words, he will close down this paper. So let's not talk about him either."

"Then how about something on that art teacher who is always making us draw abstracts of our sexual organs or that history teacher who thinks we need more Americans like John Dillinger."

Again I explained to them the realities. I told them that understanding teachers wasn't always easy, and it was best sometimes to accept what they said or did on trust. To make my point, I threw in a little Plato and told them that what one sees isn't what one sees because it's only a fragment of something larger and nobler. Then I mixed in some Hegel. "After all, if we are all a part of something greater (and as Hegel confirms, continuously evolving toward perfection) that makes us as teachers, who were chosen to guide you, very special people. Given this reality," I said in conclusion. "It's impossible for mere students to judge the superior minds of us teachers leading you to higher planes of consciousness. So it's very important that you accept our wisdom and let it just grow within you!"

Borlinda Borgia was obviously unimpressed with what I said. Before she could say something which would distract me from my course, I again addressed the group. "Now back to my original question: What should be the theme for our first issue? Remember, next month we're going to be celebrating Drug Awareness Week. Are there *any* suggestions?"

"Why not a gossip column? All papers should have a gossip column."

"Sure we can have a gossip column, but what will we talk about? What will be the *theme?*"

"How about something on whose dating who?" a girl said.

"That's a great idea," one boy responded. "I can give it a male slant and rate the girls. You know, who delivers what and how."

"That's fine, but we still need a lead article, something that will set the tone and get everyone's attention. Something. . . ."

Borlinda's hand went up. All right, I thought. Let's see what Miss Blue-Eyed-Blonde-Chastity has to say.

"Mr. Hamme. I think you hit upon an excellent idea when you mentioned Drug Awareness Week. Why just the other day on Seventh and Market, while talking to a street-corner evangelist, I saw several Horace Mann students buy drugs from the local dealer. And that isn't all. In the little lady's room, I have actually gotten dizzy inhaling some of that secondhand smoke."

"You know, Borlinda. I think you've hit upon something. That could be the *perfect* subject for our first issue. It may be exactly what we need to complement Drug Awareness Week." She beamed, delighted with my approval. That girl is going to be easier to develop than I thought. "But from what angle?" I added, leading them further into the subject.

"Mr. Hamme, I've got some connections on the street. Maybe I can do something on the local drug operation."

"Excellent, Jeremiah. Let's be like the *New York Evening Post* and publish 'All the news that's fit to print.' "

"I think that's the *Times'* motto, Mr. Hamme," Borlinda corrected.

Where does she get all her facts? She's a walking encyclopedia.

"Regardless, we must dedicate ourselves to truth, to all that's fit to print, and never forget Joe Pulitzer's famous statement, 'accuracy, accuracy, accuracy.'"

I paused, waited for more ideas, but none came. Their lack of responsiveness made them totally useless. I was about to lead them along further when Roger spoke. "Mr. Hamme, don't you think we should tell the other side of the story also? It'll make Jeremiah's article stronger."

"What do you have in mind, Roger?"

"How about something on vitamins? I could do a great piece on that subject for you."

"Don't you think that's a little *too* self-serving?"

"It could be to your advantage," he said.

"Well in that case," I smiled, pleased, "how about something on the health advantages. That would be a wonderful way of telling the other side of the story and putting everything into proper perspective." I turned to the others. "One last thing," I said. "Will someone check out *La Esperanza?* There's been a rumor that this popular student hangout has run into trouble with the government, and its business is shifting to the trendy, new Half-Moon House."

After I dismissed them, I saw Borlinda hurry to the door. When she was next to Roger, she dropped her pencil. Without saying a word, he politely retrieved it, then, after handing it to her, departed. She stood in place, as the others walked around her, and with a look of disappointment, watched him leave.

The minute I arrived Monday at school Pepe summoned me to his office. Knowing him as well as I did, I knew what the subject would be. Prepared for a long confessional, I sat in my favorite leather chair, lighted a Cuban cigar, and waited for him to pour out his heart.

"Oh, Frank," he said. "I didn't get a wink of sleep all weekend."

"Niko?" I asked.

He nodded. "How did you know?"

"It shows all over your face."

"That obvious?" he asked. I nodded. He removed a mirror from his top drawer, then examined himself. "You're right, Frank. Those bags, those bloodshot eyes. I really should wear sunglasses, but that would be too obvious. No, I think I'll just lock myself in my office and cry!"

"Was it that bad?" I said, eager for the details, certain that the very macho Niko Papalodopoulos would soon be castrated.

He sniffled, then blew his nose into a lace-trimmed handkerchief. "I think that man's going to break my heart!"

"What did that brute do to you to cause you such pain?" I said, feigning concern. "Tell me, Pepe, so that I can punch him in the mouth."

"It's what he didn't do, Frank. Our first date, it could've been so wonderful, if only he had given me a corsage, or kissed me good night, or when he took me home, escorted me to the apartment like a gentleman. But no, not Niko. He just dropped me at the curb and let me climb out of the car in my angle-length Givenchy without the slightest assistance."

"You mean he *never* touched you?" I asked pointedly.

"No," he said. "Not once. For the entire evening all he did was ask me questions. He was obsessed with knowing whom I preferred, Pepe or Pepita."

"How strange!" I said.

"I agree. If I didn't like the man so much, I would've been furious. But I absolutely *adore* him, and I wanted him to adore me too. So I told him the truth. I told him, when I was with a man, I love being Pepita. But when I was at school, I was quite comfortable being Pepe. He thought that was peculiar, and that having two identities could cause severe personality disorder."

"Oh, he's crazy," I said.

"That's what I thought too, and I told him. I said, 'Niko, I've been this way most of my life, and I've never had any problems dealing with it.' He thought that was interesting, but he still wondered if I would be happier as either Pepe or Pepita."

"You mean, have a sex change?" I asked, shocked at the thought of Pepe/Pepita without his dick or tits.

"I guess. The music was sometimes too loud, and I couldn't always hear him. Maybe I'll find out next weekend. He wants to have dinner then, but this time he wants me to come as Pepe. I guess he's trying to decide whom he likes best, Pepe or Pepita."

"You don't think he's toying with you, do you?"

"He wouldn't dare!"

"For Niko's sake, I hope you're right."

But secretly I hoped he wasn't. Niko was an arrogant subversive who deeply offended me with his anti-public school attitude. It was time he met his fate. No one was as good at revenge as Pepita. The bodies of her ex-lovers were everywhere, and, if I'm lucky, Niko will be among them.

"Stop worrying," I said, building him up for what I hoped would later be a big let down. "It's all very possible that this is his way of courting you. We men behave strangely with women we like. We don't always show them how much we care, because it may cause romantic indifference. So we use little tricks to confuse them, and keep them guessing. The object is to become their obsession. Then when they are totally committed to us, we carry them off like Lochinvar into the night. It's the old male/female courting process. I've seen it played out hundreds of times."

He thought about it for a moment, then said. "You're absolutely right." He beamed with delight. "That's got to be the reason. Why else would he have gone out with me if he weren't dazzled by my beauty?"

"Exactly."

"Oh, Frank. It's so refreshing to have a man's point of view. I feel better already."

That Italian Imposter is the most *infuriating* bitch I've ever met. How dare she continuously correct me with her inappropriate classroom remarks. Doesn't she realize who I am? If I were in England now in my rightful place next to the Queen herself, I would have her beheaded for all those unpardonable insults to a descendant of a Suscrofa. I ought to reach out and give her what virtuous ladies with her religious persuasion so desperately need. But I wouldn't dare. To cross that invisible line, which divides teachers and students, would be a breach of my professional responsibility.

What I should do—what any reasonable teacher *must* do—is provide her with a distraction.

By the way she follows Roger Murphy around the school with her Bible, it's obvious what that distraction ought to be. Unfortunately, catching a hunk like Roger isn't going to be easy. It requires more than just Christian charm. What she needs is the right look. As long as she covers what seems to be ample breasts and a good figure with loose-fitting clothes, she will always be hiding that look. If I'm ever to free myself of her unwanted classroom interferences, I will have to see to it that she shows her glory to the world.

My opportunity came, when she joined the newspaper. As my assistant, I was in the perfect position to influence her taste. During our contact, while working on *The Inquisitor,* I decided to take full advantage of the opportunity and expose her to some of my charm.

Although she seemed to behave with indifference, I knew it was only an act. Beneath that layer of indifference was a woman ready to come alive. No one knew as well as I the signs. I have seen too many men and women melt at the sight of me to be fooled by the act. And those who didn't melt at first sight melted the moment I turned on my charm. Who knew better than I the secrets of seduction? When you are as handsome as I, it comes naturally. You know exactly how to enter the room, what clothes to wear, what colognes to use. But most of all you know how to look at women without speaking to awaken them. And when they are near, as Borlinda is right now, you know what parts of their body to brush innocently with your hand. I have prepared many girls for womanhood during my years of teaching. None, though, will thrill me as much as Borlinda Borgia, the convent-trained, blue-eyed-blonde-Polack-virgin-turned-dago.

"Mr. Hamme," she said. "Jeremiah's article is terrible. It's not only illiterate, but some of it just doesn't make sense. On top of that, he even makes remarks that are libelous!"

"Let's see," I said, pulling my chair very close to hers. I then excited her senses, first with a whiff of my cologne, then with a touch of my magnificent body. Her response was instantaneous—first a sneeze, then a slap of her arm as though some pesty insect had landed there.

"What are you wearing?" she asked unexpectedly.

"Smegma Number 5," I said, pleased with my choice of colognes. "Do you like it?"

She pulled her chair away. "For repelling mosquitoes."

What's wrong with that girl? Is she like our hook-nose superintendent, beneath her veneer of innocence, another dyke? No, she can't be. I've seen the way she looks at boys. That isn't the look of a dyke, but a woman ready to sacrifice her maidenhood for a man. Nothing—not even her gold crucifix chained to her neck—can conceal the excitement men like me awaken in her.

I tried again. Again she sneezed and slapped her arm. I guess I'll just have to try another cologne on the bitch.

"The article, please," I said, grabbing the paper she was editing. I read the lead. "Wanna smoke? Then head over to *La Esperanza*. There ain't nothing you can't buy here, and many of the kids—like Chu Chu Chan and Temple Shahri—can be seen shopping here every day after school.

"There's just one problem. They ain't got safe smokes. Several kids and one teacher went on trips even to this day (three weeks later) they ain't quite returned from. I don't need to tell none of you about certain people at school. We all know what geeks they are. Well, now at least we know why. So if you really want to go up, up and away (and probably never return) head over to *La Esperanza*. For the rest of you, you might wanna head to Kelly's Half-Moon House. Now this guy has some really safe smokes at fair prices."

"You're quite right, Borlinda. It's libelous. Without proper documentation, it would be journalistically irresponsible to run it as it is." She beamed with delight, obviously proud of my approval. "So let's start by making a few deletions. But before I do any editing to this section on the Half-Moon House, find out if Kelly wants to advertise. You can have Jeremiah tell him if he wants a good editorial plug in our next issue he might want to run an ad. We're going to have to make it a firm policy at *The Inquisitor* (at least as long as I'm in charge) only paying advertisers will get free editorial space. The only exception will be in those cases when the information is an integral part of the story."

"But Mr. Hamme, you know nothing about this Half-Moon House. Don't you think you should check it out before you recommend it?"

"Don't be silly. I know all I need to know. Besides, we can't be too selective about who advertises. We need all the money we can get to finance this excellent teaching tool." I then grabbed my red pen. "Now let me show you how a real editor edits."

"But you didn't do anything!" she said after reviewing the changes. "You just deleted some names. Is that *all* you're going to do? What about the grammatical lapses? Aren't you going to correct them?"

"Borlinda," I said, remembering something I had once read by a prominent New York editor, "a good editor lets the voice of his writers surface. To edit Jeremiah's excellent piece of investigative journalism beyond what I've done would be to destroy his voice and his stylistic uniqueness."

"But it's illiterate and. . . ."

"Oh, dear Borlinda. You must forget those archaic ideas about language you learned at the Virgin Mary. In the real world, this is how *real* people write. Expecting them to be grammatical would be pretentious, and it would destroy the delicateness of their unique voice."

"But what about the contents of the article. It actually condones smoking. Is that what you want *The Inquisitor* to do?"

"Kids will be kids. So why not tell them where they can go for a safe cigarette. To be silent would be irresponsible."

"But our bodies are the Temple of the Holy Ghost," she said, stunned. "And it's a sin against Him to defile it with impurities."

"In case you aren't aware of it, every time you have a soft drink or a little tea or coffee, you are taking in caffeine. When you eat that wholesome food you buy from your favorite carry-out or have a refreshing glass of tap water, you are loading yourself with chemicals. Given this reality, how could you possible see anything wrong with an occasional smoke—especially those aromatic herbal blends? Can such cigarettes be any more impure than your food or drinks?"

She stared at me with that look of Christian superiority. "I'm going to pray for you tonight," she said. She then began to read the next article.

That girl is infuriating. Freeing that brainwashed bitch of all that Christian propaganda isn't going to be easy.

Four

Every student, after reading *The Inquisitor*, was talking about Roger's article and the vitamins he sold for a Colombian manufacturer. What made his article special was the knowledgeable way he wrote it. With considerable skill, surprising even me, he provided an in-depth look at the pill business, explaining the side-effects from excess, the health-hazards from neglect, and the pleasures from sensible use. Published with the article was a photograph of him wearing a bikini and holding a bottle of colorful pills. The photograph and article, for which I only charged him a $100 to publish, turned out to be an excellent advertisement for him. There wasn't a girl at school who didn't save the photograph and tape it to the inside of her locker door. The only exception was Borlinda. She taped the original, which she stole from the newspaper files.

Needless to say, because of this interesting article (and, of course, Jeremiah's investigative piece on *La Esperanza*), the newspaper was an immediate sell out. To meet the large demand, we had to schedule a second printing. I was so impressed with the sales potential that I decided to ask several students to approach local merchants for their assistance in distributing the paper locally. Unfortunately, this didn't work out well, because the students in their eagerness to sell distribution rights neglected to emphasize the correct sales points. Angered by what the students said, a few merchants called and complained. Fortunately, I had the presence of mind to defuse their anger and explain to them that the publication wasn't intended to be a trade paper for the drug cult (as one student so carelessly referred to it), but instead a journalistically responsible examination of drug problems and solutions. "As a public school teacher who is dedicated to serving the community by educating its young," I said to one merchant, "it is my responsibility to alert students to the alternatives to drugs. In fact, if we want them to enjoy a full and happy life, and grow up to be taxpaying, red-white-and-blue Americans just like you and me, we all must do our share by contributing to this end."

"Is that why you ran that ad with the headline: 'Come, fly the Jamaican way—see Kelly for a trip to paradise?' Or those other ads selling marijuana-leaf T-shirts and coke-spoon necklaces?"

"I see nothing wrong with such ads," I said firmly. "First of all, Kelly is a very responsible travel agent and convenience store owner who is currently offering our students a once-in-a-life-time opportunity to tour Jamaica's tobacco fields. Secondly, we are trying to keep the students' focused on the enemy, and if wearing a marijuana leaf T-shirt or a coke-spoon necklace will do it, then that's what we ought to do."

"I suppose that's also why you ran those articles you ran, especially that one on 'vitamins'?"

"As far as those articles are concerned, *especially* that excellent piece on vitamins—as I said before—I think it's time students realize what the alternative to drugs are."

Unfortunately, he didn't agree, and he reacted emotionally by slamming the phone down after calling me the Timothy Leary of the public school system. Similar behavior from other adults in the community convinced me I had created a truly brilliant first issue. Fortunately, such negative response from adults didn't discourage sales. Students from nearby schools began to cut classes just to buy a copy and get their supply of vitamins. Even several forward-thinking, elementary school principals, who recognized the newspaper's value at fighting the war on drugs, ordered issues for their schools.

"You can't imagine how excited I am," I told *The Inquisitor* staff. "Our first issue—*a sell out!* I know it's going to be difficult to top. But let's try. Let's have our next issue carry the theme the President advocates—'Squeal on Your Parents and Keep Drugs Out of the Home!'"

"Can I do another investigative piece?" Jeremiah asked.

"Certainly," I said. "But dig deeper this time, and go to the heart of the problem."

"I will, Mr. Hamme," he said. "This time I'll go right to the Jamaican connection."

Several students gasped in shock. If my guess is correct, based on student reaction, Jeremiah may have come up with a hot idea for our next issue.

Drug Awareness Week began with an assembly. The speaker selected to discuss the evils of drugs was Kelly, the local black businessman. As a public school dropout who strayed before going straight, Kelly was in Pepe's opinion the perfect person to talk to the kids about drugs. For the occasion, instead of wearing his colorful street clothes, which had become his trademark, he dressed smartly in a conservative white wool suit and matching silk tie. Resting on his shoulders was a leopard skin coat with a sable lining and collar. A huge diamond ring dominated one finger. As he strutted to the microphone, he had everyone's attention.

"Look at that ring and coat," I overheard one student say. "Man, can you imagine how many candy bars and holidays you have to sell to dress like that?"

"Shit, what I wouldn't give to have some of his dough," another student replied.

The speaker who was at least four feet taller than the microphone waited center-stage for the conversation to cease. When he had total silence, he turned to his left and snapped his fingers. A voluptuous, white woman stepped onto the stage. She was wearing a tight, red mini-dress, which kept creeping up when she walked. To prevent a public scandal by allowing the skirt to rise too high, she would pause every few steps to straighten it. The sight of her in motion— wiggling her hips while straightening her skirt—filled the auditorium with whistles and comments. When she reached center-stage, she gave everyone a front, side, and rear Hollywood, glamour-girl view of herself. After delighting the audience for few moments with her wiggles and heavy breathing, she removed the speaker's coat, and walked slowly off stage without once attempting to straighten the skirt. Her decision to let it rise got a standing ovation.

All the heads reluctantly returned to the speaker who waited patiently for silence. "When I was asked to talk to you today," he said, bending forward to speak into the mike, "I at first refused. What could I say? What advice could I give you to discourage you from making the same mistakes I had? Then it dawned on me. I could tell you the truth. Who was better able to tell you about the fast life than me? For five years, I made more money than I could spend. I lived better than a king with jet planes, villas, and great friends all over the world."

He then went into detail regarding his negotiations with international dealers, his clashes with Colombian distributors, and his secret arrangements with U.S. officials for local distribution rights for his Jamaican tobacco. In telling us about himself, he revealed the life of a man who lived on the edge of danger—of a man who was always a moment ahead of disaster. It was an exciting life, a James Bond life of fast cars, fast women and fast money. There wasn't a single student in the auditorium who wasn't totally impressed.

"But despite all the money and glamour," he continued, "it wasn't a real life. Many a night I would ask myself: Why didn't I follow my teachers' advice? Why didn't I finish high school and go on to college? Despite all my worldly success, I still needed something more, something real. I *needed* an education. So my advice to you. Get yourself an education, and enjoy a sensible life as a teacher or a computer operator or an accountant. Don't be like me and waste yourself in the fast lane. It leads no where, and one day—maybe after it's too late (or if you're lucky like me, before it's too late)—you'll wake up and say: Why didn't I listen to my teachers? Why didn't I go on to college?"

At the end of the assembly, students mobbed him and brazenly asked him how they could make money too. Among the students was Roger Murphy.

"You want to make money?" he said privately to them. "Then come to my seminar Saturday." And he slipped them his business card, which I also took by pushing my arm through the wall of students. "I'm always interested in finding recruits who are willing to stay in school and make some quick cash!"

Pepe scheduled two more assemblies, one Tuesday and another Wednesday. At both assemblies, a movie was shown. The first movie was about a white boy of Eastern European origin who was introducing a black Hispanic boy to the world of "kiddie drugs." The movie began with an informative scene in which the white boy led the Hispanic through the supermarket. He was pointing out different aerosol cans and telling the Hispanic what a snort from each would do. And the movie ended with a dramatic scene in which the Hispanic, while sniffing the contents of an aerosol can, suddenly stopped breathing.

The look of joy on his face before his death was almost identical to the look I noticed on my students' faces after taking their vitamins.

Although it was a good movie, it was nevertheless booed, because of the ending. The students obviously felt as I had, that the Hispanic should have lived to enjoy a better life. I would have loved to have seen the two boys turn straight like Kelly and visit the schools where they could share their experiences with others.

What made this movie important was its message about which inhalants to avoid and why. An Oscar should have been given to those two reformed drug users for so successfully portraying the tragedy of two kids who carelessly went on a sniffing spree in a supermarket.

As often as I had seen the movie, I still learned something new from it each time. It really makes me furious to think businessmen are getting rich selling such harmful products to teenagers. I must remember to write my senator and encourage him to support a law forbidding businessmen from selling kids such products. The money raised from cleverly entrapping the law breakers could then be spent on more drug awareness programs like this one.

After seeing the movie, the students began to show a concern about all the aerosol cans at school. As quickly as they found them (in purses, lockers, and desk drawers), they emptied them (to prevent abuse) before discarding them. The only person who wasn't pleased was the janitor who had to pick up all the discarded cans. When I told him how proud I was of the students for volunteering to empty the cans so no one could use them, he merely looked at me strangely, then walked away.

The second movie dealt with children born to crack-smoking parents. Most movies, focusing on the effects of drugs on the innocent, became clinical and dull. This one, though, was refreshingly entertaining. From the moment the credits appeared, we were quickly pulled into the exciting world of hyperactive children. Seeing those darlings reminded me of playful monkeys swinging and leaping over obstacles. Although none could speak, they all managed to make raucous sounds, not too unlike baboons mating. One girl, protected in her playpen from the others, was particularly endearing. While all the kids around her were in continuous motion, she sat in her playpen and arranged blocks. In the middle of building a pyramid, she suddenly stopped, scratched her head, then stared at the blocks in confusion, as though she had Alzheimer's and had forgotten what she was doing. Frustrated at being unable to remember, she violently slapped the blocks, knocking them all down, then burst into tears.

To provide a focus, the movie featured two very person-able children, Rachel and Gunter. Rachel, whose nervous system was damaged by crack while in the womb, was born without feeling. This tragedy was conveyed in an excellent scene in which she fell and broke her arm. Instead of crying, as most children would, she merely got up and walked away, carrying her broken arm, twisted out of shape, as though nothing was wrong. To protect Rachel from future injuries her adoptive parents wisely locked her in a padded cage where she amused herself beating her cloth animals against the floor.

But it was Gunter who stole the movie. Watching this energetic four-year-old bump into walls, trip over nothing, and fall to the floor while trying to sit in a chair, filled the auditorium with laughter. In one especially amusing scene, while eating mashed potatoes, he missed his mouth and hit his nose. The unhappy look on his face, the tears in his eyes, made the moment *absolutely* charming.

It wasn't until near the end that the movie got serious. Then the focus switched to the schools, and how they should deal with hyperactive children. Recommended were class-rooms with padded walls and pillow-filled rest areas and jungle-gym-like apparatus. Teachers would no longer teach the three Rs, but would instead start teaching basic social skills through play. The annual cost to implement these changes was estimated at $15,000 per student, which was only $10,000 more per year than it was currently costing tax-payers. But when you consider all the special training teach-ers needed and all the special equipment the schools needed, this all seemed like so little for such an important job.

When the movie was over, I applauded the artistic skill with which the director made his point about how impor-tant it was for pregnant women to avoid crack. Because of the entertaining way it was done, I was optimistic about the movie's potential for commercial success when nationally released. There was only one problem: The movie had cast a negative light on crack. I must remember to write the pro-ducer and remind him that crack—though unacceptable for pregnant women—could still serve a social usefulness. Stud-ies have confirmed that when crack was taken in lieu of the more expensive recreational drugs, crime dropped signifi-cantly in major urban areas. Therefore, crack should be fea-tured as an inexpensive solution to social problems in cities seriously affected by heavy crime, *not the problem!*

The war on drugs didn't end with the assemblies. Each teacher was asked to incorporate the subject into his lesson. In the art class students drew pictures of the drug experi-ence, in the music class they sang popular songs about drugs, in the science class they learned how drugs were made, in the social studies class they mapped the international drug routes, and in the English class, they read poems, stories, and essays by former drug addicts. If John Dewey were liv-ing today, he would have been proud of the way Pepe had orchestrated this magnificent Drug Awareness Program.

For Borlinda's benefit, I introduced my class to the Rastafarians of Jamaica who were well-known for their use of *ganja*. By following the dietary laws of the Bible, they found many practical uses for *ganja*—like smoking it in their water pipes, drinking it as a medicinal tea, and cooking it with their vegetables. To document their Biblical base for their actions, I quoted some key passages in the Bible which supported the Rastas position. (Genesis 3:18, "and thou shall eat the herb of the field." Psalms 104:14, "He causeth the grass to grow for the cattle, and herb for the service of man.") My purpose was to alert Borlinda to the hedonistic passages in the Bible. It pleased me to see her check her Bible to verify.

"So you see, class," I said solemnly, speaking directly to Borlinda. "Even the Bible recommends a little psychedelic stimulation. So maybe it's best you don't heed its advice—unless you want to produce kids like those we just saw in the movies."

It was obvious that Borlinda didn't agree, but it was also obvious that she had the good sense not to argue with me. My grasp of the Scriptures was proving to be too considerable for her. A few more lectures like this, and she will be coming to me for advice.

Oh what putty these children are in my skilled hands!

Five

Pepe was right. The vitamins did make a difference. Since Roger had begun selling his pills in class, I noticed a significant improvement in the attitude of the seniors. They now listened to my lectures with the dazed, open-mouth look of children staring at their creator in wonderment. Seeing them, so ready and alert, delighted me. In a just matter of a few days, I was able to make contact with them.

Borlinda was the exception, at least until yesterday. By silencing her, as I had, with my knowledge of the Bible, I had forced her to recognize my intellectual superiority. Confident of my breakthrough, I decided to prepare her for the next phase of her education and discuss sex in literature. As a Virgin Mary dropout, she was obviously lacking in this area. This meant that I would have to open her eyes to its elemental importance. After all, I was a Renaissance public school teacher, whose students were wiser and more experienced than other students, and I wasn't going to allow one Virgin Mary dropout to ruin my reputation by graduating from Horace Mann unprepared for the joys of life.

For so many people (particularly the majority) sex is such an important catalyst to Truth. It is only through sharing strong physical union with others that they can glimpse the

Light. Some lucky few like me, on the other hand, seldom need sex, because we *are* Truth. The only time we seek sex is to deepen our understanding of some extremely abstract revelation.

Since sex is so urgent, particularly for adolescent boys and girls, not using it to advance important concepts would, as a teacher, be irresponsible. Pepe was so wise to stress at faculty meetings the need for teachers to make their lectures relevant. Whenever I am in conflict with the kids, because I expect more than they can deliver, whenever I can't quite push them to higher levels of learning, because they lack sufficient brain cells, I quickly reduce everything to the physical and watch little explosions occur (sometimes in the boys' pants). At such times, I am proud that I am a teacher, that I have been chosen to teach at this great school where the best are mine to lead.

For Borlinda's sake, I began today's lecture by summarizing a few stories from the Bible. I told the class about Sodom and Gomorrah, David and Bathsheba, then finished it off with the secrets of David and Jonathan. "Great books, including the Bible," I said to the class, remembering what I had read in an adult book store magazine, "have always had their share of sex—I think of *Portnoy's Complaint*, *Fear of Flying*, *Looking for Mr. Goodbar*, and for you boys with a gay bent, that excellent piece of French naughtiness, *Our Lady of the Flowers*. But my favorite book, one that I insist you all read, is *Les Liaisons Dangereuses*," and I then went to the blackboard and wrote the title, forming my letters in my distinctive script, with just enough fuss to be elegant. "This is one book that won't disappoint you. The main characters in this delightful little tale turn love into such a sophisticated art. Their romantic escapades will enrich your life in ways you'll never forget. For you nonreaders, I *strongly* recommend you rent the video. The same applies to other titles we will discuss from time to time. In fact, I think I might just include on my reading list the names of books available on video. Now it must never be forgotten. Hollywood is not always responsible in its transformation of books to movies, and it has been known to make some fatal artistic changes. But you will find, as I have learned, that despite these changes Hollywood still manages to express important truths through film. Never forget. No matter how well a writer writes about love *nothing* compares to a good close-up camera shot.

"Today's lecture will be based on two fascinating love stories, Somerset Maugham's *Rain*, and Nathaniel Hawthorne's *The Scarlet Letter*. Since I prefer the character of Sadie Thompson to Hester Prynne, I will focus primarily on *Rain*. It is shorter and easier to read, and it is something that I can easily cover in the remaining time. Those of you who decide to read *The Scarlet Letter* will find that Hester's development lacks sexual tension. Maugham, on the other hand, doesn't make this fatal mistake. His development of Sadie, that floozy from Honolulu, is direct and exciting."

I then told them about Sadie's South Sea adventure (and, if I must admit, with the skill of a Somerset Maugham). After describing the conflict between Sadie and the missionary, I delivered the missionary's famous line, after she repented, and summed up her future now that she would be deported to San Francisco. I delivered the lines with all the righteous pleasure of the missionary. I wanted the class to understand the joy he derived from committing this happy lady to a life of hell in a California prison.

"She's sinned," I said in my most dramatic voice, "and for that sinning, she must suffer. I know what she'll endure. There will be starvation, torture, *humiliation!* Nevertheless, I want her to experience this. I want her to accept this experience joyfully, as a sacrifice to God. After all, this is a rare opportunity offered only to very few." Then in the voice of an angel singing praises to heaven, I added: *"Oh, isn't God good and merciful?"*

The class was horrified, everyone, that is, except Borlinda. She was pleased, because it reinforced her naive notion of divine retribution.

I let her enjoy this moment, even gloat in it, then when I felt the time was ripe, I gnashed her pleasure by focusing on what wasn't said in the story, and skillfully began to provide insight into the complex character of the missionary. "Beneath that veneer of piety was another man," I said. "It took a woman like Sadie, a Woman of the World, to uncover him. With all the talents of her profession, she seduced him, as Eve seduced Adam, and she watched him yield. In that moment, in which they had become one, she discovered a Truth, a Truth so great that it changed her life forever. She discovered that this missionary who had dedicated his life to saving sinners wasn't one of the chosen." I then cried out joyously for the entire world to hear. "Instead he was just another human in need of *her* salvation!" Then with sadness, I lowered my voice and said, "Unfortunately, he wasn't strong enough to accept Truth and like Sadie take the next step to freedom and happiness." I went to the board and wrote: "Truth must be confronted unencumbered if you want to soar like an angel to heaven." I then called on Amo to read the line for everyone to appreciate.

"Truth must be con-front-ed un-en-," he read, breaking unfamiliar words into syllables.

"Are you sounding out the words?" I asked, shocked. He nodded, embarrassed. "Haven't they taught you anything in school? You're supposed to guess! Now try that word again."

"Uninvited," he said quickly.

"Close," I said. "It's unencumbered." I then read the sentence to them, afraid that they might miss the point if they depended on Amo's reading for an understanding. As I completed my lecture, my gaze settled on Borlinda who was obviously in thought.

"You're immoral," Borlinda blurted out indignantly, when our gazes met.

I sat on the edge of my desk, crossed my legs, and squeezed. "No, Borlinda," I said. "I'm not immoral. I'm amoral. There's a difference. Immoral presupposes a right and wrong, but amoral doesn't. You see, Borlinda, I live in the real world, the world *beyond* man's limited experiential boundaries. I live in the spiritual world of the Ideal. In such a world, there is no such thing as right and wrong, because we are all a part of something larger and greater. Personally, Borlinda I think it's time you liberate yourself and step into this world. As Auntie Mame sang out in that great Broadway show, you must open a new door. So open a new door, Borlinda. . . ."

I suddenly spread my legs and revealed my thinly veiled serpent, confident and ready. "And live!" I said, rising to my feet to emphasize the moment with my physical superiority. "You've got to live, Borlinda. *Live!*" The class gasped. There wasn't one girl in that room who wasn't ready for me. There wasn't one boy in that room whom my male superiority did not intimidate. I was in control. Those pimpled-faced, confused little twits were mine again, and I did it by just showing my grandeur. Even Borlinda responded. I could hear her breathing quicken and feel her stare grow intense. She was breaking, yielding, the woman within her was about to spring free.

Then she surprised me. When I thought I had reached the woman in the girl, when I was sure I had finally made an impression and touched the secret to her joy, she rose. "I don't know about the rest of the class," Borlinda said. "But I'd rather suffer the affliction with the people of God than to enjoy the pleasures of sin for even a season." She then left the room, taking with her her nimbus, which gave her a look of radiant divinity.

That one is a real pain in the ass!

I was just about ready to enjoy a herbal cigarette Roger had left me, when a middle-aged duplication of Borlinda came to the door. Like Borlinda, she wore no makeup and dressed in practical, loose-fitting clothes.

Borlinda pointed toward me. "That's the one, mother. That's the one I've been telling you about."

The woman approached me with the no-nonsense attitude of a professional virgin in complete control of her libido. En route she examined me from head to toe, pausing briefly in-between, before jerking her head up. Her fiery, word-of-God blue eyes locked with mine, and she dared me, by her look to pull away. "I'm Mrs. Borgia. My daughter tells me shocking things about you. Are you aware of the wages of sin?"

"Mrs. Borgia, I am very well aware of the Wages of Sin. In fact, that's why I teach. I want to protect my students from making mistakes with their lives."

"That isn't what my daughter tells me. She thinks you are trying to do just the opposite."

"True, on the surface, some of my views are a little untraditional for the ecclesiastical. Still, that all changes once you understand my philosophic purpose. You see within my somewhat worldly facade is a very religious man, a man concerned about the spiritual development of each of his students. In fact, within all my lessons, I make it a point to plant spiritual truths that will help my students grow. Last term, for example, several of my students really benefited from my guidance. There was Igor Ivanovich who has gone on to star in several really exciting art film, and Tom Wong who. . . ."

"Don't believe him, mother. He's a devil in disguise."

I'm going to burn that girl's Bible if she doesn't shut up.

"Now, now Borlinda. Didn't I today discuss the religious conflicts of several prominent characters in the Bible? Didn't I also try to enlarge your spiritual awareness of great literature? You wrong me, Borlinda. For some reason, you ignore my larger purpose and seem only concerned about the narrowest point of my lectures."

"My daughter told me in detail about some of those *narrow* points as well as your *larger* purpose. I'll have you know Borlinda is a fine Christian girl, and she isn't accustomed to such inappropriate behavior and comments from others, *especially* teachers. Before her father died she was an honor student at the Virgin Mary Bible Academy, but because of lack of funds, I had to enroll her in the public schools. Just because she's here (in this *den of corruption*), doesn't mean she has abandoned all decency and goodness. In fact, I have taught her to cling to it tenaciously, as a defense against all the evil around her."

"You must forgive me, Mrs. Borgia, for defending myself, but I hardly think of my English class, or this fine school, as a den of corruption. My life has been devoted to helping young men and women resist the wickedness of the world so that they can soar like angels to Paradise."

She yanked a copy of *The Inquisitor* from her purse, then shoved it into my face. "Is this how you want them to soar? On the wings of hallucinogens?"

Once again I launched into my talk about the Fifth Amendment (First Amendment, Borlinda corrected), and the right of the students to express themselves. "My responsibility, as a teacher, is to allow each of my students to become independent individuals with their own special voice. To crush this voice before it could be heard would be to destroy life without giving it a chance to grow. True, the newspaper lacks significant insights. But this is only a high school, and they are only teenagers. Someday through experience and hard work this will all change for them. By permitting them the freedom to express themselves, I am giving them the opportunity to discover Truth and experience true spiritual happiness."

"Oh, dear God," Borlinda said suddenly, looking quite pale. "Deliver us from this man."

"My daughter is correct," Mrs. Borgia said. "Ye have sinned against the Lord. Be sure your sins will find you out!" Her gaze, which was locked with mine, unexpectedly lowered. "And I intend to see to it personally." She stiffened, then threw her head back. "Come, Borlinda. It's time we talk to the principal."

As I watched them leave, I knew that mother, with Borlinda as her informer, was going to be one very serious problem. My last run-in with an angry parent for daring to lead his daughter to the Light resulted in my being forced to resign from my job. If this occurred again and became a pattern, it could ruin my fine reputation and even make me unemployable.

The loss to education would be immeasurable. Without me, who would lead these kids to the Light? *Who could?* This great school, which the President created to be a model for *my* type of *avant-garde* teaching, would crumble to its foundation. For the sake of the President, the public schools, the future of America, I must *never* permit this. The hope for all our schools rests on my shoulders—*on my checking those two uptight, sanctimonious, Bible freaks!*

I think it's time I see Pepe. It's time I get some of his wisdom, and learn exactly what he feels needs to be done to stop those two bitches before they get out of control.

When I was just about ready to leave, Niko arrived. He stood by the door and, for a moment, resembled one of those half-man, half-beast creatures from mythology, demented queens like Pepe/Pepita went crazy over. There was an amused twinkle in his eye, which unexpectedly spread across his face when his gaze settled on the wall containing the publicity posters from several of my favorite movies—*Cleopatra's Passion*, *The Marquise de Sade*, and *Hitler's Secret Love*.

He withheld laughing. "I see you like X-rated classics."

"Very much," I said, impressed with his ability to recognize the educational importance of those movies. "As a Renaissance teacher, I always try to expose my students to the important side of the great men and women in history. Films like those are excellent teaching tools. I've seen them many times, and I am quite pleased with the accuracy with which they portray the true passions of those men and women in history!"

He didn't reply. He just shook his head, then glanced at the wall near my desk where my coat of arms and degrees hung, and smiled. "Well, I must admit your classroom isn't too much different from what I had expected."

"Is that why you came? To study a master teacher's classroom?"

"That's one reason," he said. "I did want to see the room where the brilliant Hamme dazzled the senior class with his wit and intelligence five hours a day."

"Now that you have," I said, suspecting a sarcastic edge to his remark, "what's the other reason for coming?"

"To again ask you to resign."

"You want *me*, Frank Hamme, to resign?" I said, amused.

"That's right," he said.

"Hasn't it sunk into your thick head that I'm not going to? When are you going to realize I'm like a fresh breeze here that opens young minds to the universe? Do you think for a moment I will relinquish my influence and quit? If anyone should quit, it's you. I know what you're doing with those kids. They talk and tell me things. Haven't you learned yet that it's against nature to teach kids to think? If the gods wanted them to think, they would have given them brains."

"You're absolutely right, Frank. We must never teach thinking skills, not if we want space cadets like that Shakespearean porn star. After all, that would go against the Divine Plan according to Hamme."

"You don't approve of the public schools, do you?"

"I don't approve of you. What you do is criminal," he said. "Your vulgar display of your anatomy, your perverse preoccupation with sex is an affront to every decent teacher in America. This is a classroom. You're supposed to be an English teacher. Not some psychopathic exhibitionist who gets his thrills corrupting young minds with pornographic passages from literature."

"*How dare you judge me!* Who gives you that right, *you*, a mere Greek of *questionable* ancestry? I exist, and will always exist, because I am a *Hamme*. When I cease, you can be certain there'll be other Hammes to continue my work, and it will be so as long as we have the public schools."

"You really are a lunatic. No wonder Borlinda and her mother are so upset with you."

"Did those two Polacks put you up to this?"

"If, by that, you mean, have I spoken to the Borgias. The answer is yes. I promised them that I would talk to you. But I don't think talking to you would do any good. The only thing that would work with you would be public exposure."

I looked at him coldly. "Mr. Papalodopoulos," I said. "Is that a threat?"

"Yes, Mr. Hamme with the silent 'E'," he said. "It *is* a threat. So remember, I'm watching you, and one slip up and I'll let the world know what a nut you are." He then left with the elegance of a gorilla swinging from a tree limb.

So that Greek wants to play rough. Trying to sabotage modern education by teaching thinking skills isn't enough. He wants to force me out of the system as well. Well, if he thinks that's going to be easy, he's in for a big surprise. I'll show him what rough is. I'll get that raging queen to take care of him. Two can play hardball!

Pepe was outside the counselor's office, straightening the announcements on the bulletin board, when I located him. He obviously wasn't paying much attention to what he was doing. Bulletins were hung upside down; words were misspelled, and every time someone passed in the hall he turned expectantly to greet him.

When I approached him (with my distinctively male gait), he swung around on his toes, as though he were waltzing to Strauss, and flashed the happiest, gayest smile. But when he saw me, his smile became a frown, and he fell back on his heels with a thump.

"Oh, Frank," he said. "You are determined to make my life hell."

"Then you spoke to the Borgias?"

He nodded. "Now that is one *angry* woman."

"I know," I said, concerned. "What are we going to do about her?"

"I've already done all I can. I listened to her. I poured out my concern. I assured her that I would talk with you. Then, I recommended that she see Phyl Jaffe for her thoughts on the matter."

"Why on earth would you send her to that bull. . . ."

"Now, now. No names. Phyl has changed. She's become a very religious person, and the two of them should get along famously. Besides, it doesn't hurt to get a woman's point of view. Phyl has worked with parents like Mrs. Borgia before and knows exactly what to do. So we must be sensible now, and leave it to Phyl."

"But what am I going to do about Borlinda? That girl's impossible."

"You're just going to have to accelerate her education," he said, leading me down the hall, away from Niko's office. "Now enough about them. Let me tell you about my date Saturday night. Let me tell you what that *brute* Niko did."

I suspected Pepe was ready for the truth, and it was time to start planting in his susceptible mind *exactly* what Niko was!

"Has that Greek Neanderthal been trifling with your heart?" I said, sounding sympathetic. "Oh, Pepe, I knew he wasn't the man for you."

"You're wrong, Frank. He's quite the man for me. It's just that he confuses me. During our entire date last weekend, instead of complimenting me even once, he spends all evening drilling me, asking me crazy questions like: 'How does it feel to be Pepe? Is it the same as when I am Pepita? Which persona do I prefer—Pepe or Pepita'?" Pepe sighed. "Doesn't that man understand? I am Pepe *and* Pepita, and it will always be that way. I wanted to get up and leave him, but he was sitting there, looking so handsome and butch in his slacks and sweater, that I just stayed and kept hoping he would look across the table and see me, and want me as much as I wanted him."

"Did he?" I asked pointedly.

"No," he said flatly. "He took me home and said, 'See you Monday.' Then drove off on his motorcycle, leaving me standing at the curb with a broken heart."

"What are you going to do?" I said. "You aren't going to let him hurt you like that, are you?"

"What *can* I do?"

"What you've always done," I said. "Show him your stuff, and if he doesn't deliver—*chop off his balls!*"

"Can't I show a *little* mercy?"

"You never did before. Why change now?"

"But I love him."

"There will be other men. Better men. Trust me."

"Of course, you're right. You're always right, Frank. That's why I need you as a friend. You really *do* understand."

"You're quite a woman, Pepita."

She affectionately fondled her breasts. "You noticed?"

I smiled, delighted. I knew I no longer needed to worry about Niko. Pepe would make certain to that. All I had to do was provide him with the right encouragement and the rest would be history. With the skill of a surgeon, Pepe would see to it that that descendant of that pot-bellied, undeodorized *moussaka* cook was properly neutered.

That just leaves Borlinda to worry about. How will I ever tame that one? I've tried everything from dazzling her with my manly stuff to my brilliant dissertation on literature. Nothing works. Her mind has been hermetically sealed. Even a blow torch can't open it.

Obviously I need help. It's time I call on Erda Von Schwantz.

Erda was an overweight, motherly black woman who taught sex education. For six hours a day, she was the school's authority on deviant behavior. Whenever anyone on the staff had a question on teenage disorder, they could always count on her for the answer.

Her prodigious knowledge impressed me. But what truly impressed me was how she so expertly obtained it. With the skill of a psychologist, she mismatched students in class, delivered provocative lessons, then observed reactions. When a student behaved in disgust or fascination, no matter how subtle, she noted it in context. After collecting this data, she tested it, until she understood exactly what it meant. What made her so good was her ability to step into the minds of each student and identify their unique needs, then catalog them for future reference. She took her work seriously, and gave considerable attention to the revealing details that identified patterns. The public schools, according to her, weren't a place to teach knowledge, but a place to do clinical research for the government at a profit. Because of her dedication and exceptional skill, her reports were eagerly sought. In a very short time, she made the world aware of such interesting teenage disorders as incest, necrophilia, and bestiality.

Pepe, of course, deserved some credit for Erda's success. Many of her studies were published by Pepe's university friends who were doing government research on deviant behavior (which seems to be such a growing area of interest among political types). For arranging these little deals for Erda, Pepe received a generous commission. In fact, he told me privately (and threatened to castrate me if I ever said a word about it) that he made enough money from each of these deals to buy several fabulous gowns and wigs.

What made Erda valuable—the real key to her success—was her sweet motherly attitude. Students felt comfortable opening up to such a liberated, understanding black mother, because she gave them approval, when their own mothers showed rage. Yet, also like a good mother, she would reprimand them when they were foolish and shake a finger at them, saying: "You're going to get a social disease if you don't protect yourself."

The woman was a real pro, and I deeply respected her. It's a pity my professional respect wasn't enough, and she needed more. As a full and ready woman, she saw me for what I was, a desirable man with an enormous talent, whom she needed to inflame. I warned her often that she shouldn't try. I could be more man than she could handle. Yet she always insisted. As much as I wanted to talk to her privately about Borlinda, I didn't dare. I knew what would follow.

She must have sensed my need to talk. One day while lingering outside her classroom, a big black arm reached out from the opened door, grabbed me by the collar, and pulled me into the empty classroom. "Well, hello Frank," Erda said, acting surprised at what she had caught. "How nice of you to stop by and visit me" She quickly closed the door, locked it, then dropped the key between her breasts.

"Well, I. . . ."

"Your bashfulness is so cute," she said, turning on her femininity. "You don't need to be embarrassed, you naughty boy. I know what you want." She moved toward me like some sensuous, but overweight animal moving in on her prey. I stepped backwards slowly. "You don't have to run from me, Frank," she said. "Let Erda hug you and put you out of your misery."

"I'd rather talk, Erda. *Please!*"

My back collided into the file cabinet. Erda kept me pressed against it with the full pressure of her large body. She was adorable, full of womanly affection. "Well, let's talk."

"It's about Borlinda."

"You aren't interested in that bitch, are you?" she said, disappointed. She then shook her chubby finger at me. "You're going to get into trouble playing with young girls."

"You misunderstand. I never touch my students. Once they have me, they lose control, and can't stop. So I've. . . ."

"I love your modesty, Frank," she said sweetly. "Now tell me the truth. Why are you so interested in Borlinda?"

"I just want to open her up to the joys of life, introduce her to the human race. *Free her!*"

"That's expecting a lot," Erda said.

"I know," I said. "That's why I'm turning to you. I need your help, Erda. *Desperately!* Everything I say that girl corrects. She is always staring at me with that look of disapproval. No one but you can penetrate that mind of hers and unlock it. No one here has your skill and patience."

"I don't know, Frank. That's expecting a lot. That girl's impenetrable."

"I could be very grateful if you tried."

"*Very grateful?*" she smiled. "I like that. I like that very much."

I suddenly became her entire focus. Nothing I could do could kill the desire that now filled her. She grabbed me by the head, buried my face in her perfumed breasts, then smothered me by holding me there with a mighty hug. For a moment, I thought I would lose consciousness, as she squirmed with delight. "Oh, Frank, you realize you're asking a lot," she said. She was obviously intoxicated with her power over me, while I struggled vainly for air. "You realize you are demanding skills from me that I don't have, skills that I may never have. How can I, Erda Von Schwantz, ever live up to the expectations of a Hamme?"

I tried to free myself, but my struggle only increased her pleasure and her hold on me. When she squeezed almost all the life from me, she let go and I slid to the floor, with my back against the file cabinet. "Oh Frank," she said, her hand diving into the valley of the breasts for the key. "I hope I succeed for Borlinda's sake—for *our* sake!"

She threw the key toward me. I crawled to pick it up. Gasping for air, I hurried to the door, then to my classroom for safety.

Six

Without notice in the middle of the day, a group of well-armed men broke into the *La Esperanza,* then sprayed it with bullets. According to television reports, these unidentified masked men with automatic guns entered *La Esperanza* in gangland style, shooting. After the last shot was heard, they warmed the cold winter day with a flame that devoured the building instantly.

Everyone was talking about the raid, but no one could provide an acceptable explanation for it. Occasionally I would overhear a student comment about how the Jamaicans had given it to the Colombians. But such comments made no sense to me. I could only conclude that they weren't talking about *La Esperanza,* but instead about something they were studying in history. The only people who had any information about the raid were those IRS employees conducting it. But they'd never talk. If they did, they might ruin the IRS's reputation for being obtuse and capricious, which could cause Americans to lose respect for it.

Although two Horace Mann students were killed, while purchasing medication from the pharmacist, I felt no sympathy for them. Didn't I do what any conscientious editor ought to do and warn them to avoid *La Esperanza*? I was in the newspaper office, preparing an editorial to this effect, when Erda Von Schwantz entered, then locked the door. She moved slowly toward me like an overweight, sensuous black panther, stalking prey.

"It's payday, Frank," she said.

"What do you mean, *payday?*" I said, disturbed by the wild look in her eyes.

"Have you forgotten your promise already?"

"Look Schwantz, what *are* you talking about?"

"Watch it, Frank," she said, shaking a finger at me. "That's a good German name. Don't you start using it literally."

"Then get to the point."

"Very well," she said. "I'm here, because of Borlinda."

"What about Borlinda?"

"She's changed."

"In what way?"

"Let's just say," Erda smiled, all white teeth and dimples, "I've inspired her to become more godlike."

"That's an improvement?!"

"Believe me, Frank, one look and you'll agree. That girl's on her way to paradise! Thanks to my skills, she and Roger will be making music together in no time. Borlinda with her piety, and Roger with his kinky sophistication. It'll be the love of the ages. Two irreconcilable souls pulled together to self-destruct in each other's arms. Why it brings tears to my eyes, remembering my first love. The joy, the passion, *the pain. . . ."*

She suddenly stopped reminiscing and yanked me to my feet by my hair. I was reminded of my elementary school teacher—a woman of dedication and strength who taught me respect, honor, decency. I wanted to fall to my knees before this Amazon Woman in worship. Instead, she buried my face in her perfumed breasts, and cried out: "Drink deeply, Frank, and enjoy the Pierian spring." As her perfume filled my lungs like ether, I began to fight wildly for my freedom, kicking and scratching. "That's it, Frank," she said, smothering my resistance with a tighter hold. "*I love it* when you're wild."

When I no longer had any strength, during that precious moment between life and death, while struggling for what I was sure would be my last breath, I had a magnificent spiritual experience. I saw the heavenly gates open and heard the angels sing. As I was about ready to fly off to join them, she let go, and I fell back into a chair, gasping for air.

"What a disappointment you are," she said sadly. "I thought you had more fire. But look at you. Spent before I even got started. Well, at least we tried. We can always say we tried, can't we Frank?"

I just nodded, unable to speak, as I gasped for air.

What a woman! I thought, after recovering. *What a woman!* How many can do what she just did—*and reject me?*

When Borlinda entered the classroom, everyone stopped talking and stared. Like the others, I was stunned. I had never expected Erda to achieve in such a short time such a major transformation. Although Borlinda still looked like a blue-eyed-blonde-Angel-of-God, she now looked like one who was negotiating with the devil. Her womanliness, once hidden under loose clothes, was boldly emphasized, thanks to the Body Shop Clothiers. She paused by the door so that everyone could study her, as she mischievously promoted her main attraction: her two *huge* breasts! Seeing her stand there, looking so ripe and ready, had every male, including myself, rising to the occasion—and every female *absolutely* hating her!

But it wasn't just her appearance. Her entire attitude changed. She was an extrovert, full of sparkle, with a song in her voice. She greeted her friends with religious rejoicing, full of hallelujahs, amens, and praises to the Lord. She didn't walk with her usual stride, but because of her tight skirt, she minced and pendulated to her chair. Standing by her desk, she began to fuss with her makeup. When she was finished preening, she slowly slid into her seat with just the right swing to her hips to set everything in motion, from her curly blonde hair to her perfectly shaped legs. I knew if I didn't compliment her and bring this show to an end she was going to be impossible all period.

"You've changed," I said suddenly.

"It's God's wish," she said

"You mean Erda Von Schwantz, don't you?"

"Don't be sacrilegious, Mr. Hamme. I mean, *God!* Ms. Von Schwantz just wisely explained to me that my body was the temple of the Holy Ghost, and it was a sin to hide it. God did the rest by showing me the way."

"I'm glad He did. You will make a lot of people happy."

"I hope so. Because I am going to use it to preach the word of God to the world."

At that point, there was a shift of movement from the rear to the front of the room, as the boys hurried forward to claim vacant chairs near and around Borlinda. Borlinda didn't seem to notice them. She removed her hand mirror, and became engrossed in her reflection. She smiled, after putting her mirror away, at seeing one boy stare at her with his mouth open. She removed a tract from her purse, then gave it to him.

To appeal to the new Borlinda, I decided to talk about Robert Browning's poem, "Pippa Passes." For this lecture, I concealed my manliness by sitting behind my desk. When I spoke, it was in my ecclesiastical voice, full of truth, beauty, and enough piety to turn a classroom into a sanctuary.

"Nowhere in poetry," I said in my strong baritone voice, "has a more beautiful creature than Pippa ever been created. This little Child of God, just by singing her songs, was miraculously able to change everyone she met and save them from their despair. You may ask how could she do this? How could one person so young—younger than many of you—through just the singing of songs so deeply touch the lives of so many people? Because," I said, "she had the Word of God on her side. Because," I added significantly, "'*God's in his heaven and all's right with the world.*'"

During my entire lecture, I had Borlinda's full attention. She sat in the front row and folded her hands on her Bible, as though she were in church, listening to her pastor, while the boys stared at her and drooled and the girls stared at her and fumed. Every now and then she would startle me (and the class) with an amen or hallelujah. When the lecture was over and the bell rang, she came to my desk.

"That has got to be the finest lecture I've ever heard. My English teacher at the Virgin Mary also said wonderful things about that poem, but she could never match your sensitive depth. Oh, Mr. Hamme. You've been such an inspiration today, and have lifted the burden of doubt from my shoulders with that wonderful message. I really feel ashamed questioning you. You've changed my whole opinion of you with just one lecture."

"Why thank you, Borlinda. I am so pleased you approve, because deep down, when you strip away the rhetoric, I think we are both alike, you and me."

"I wouldn't go that far," she said cautiously.

"You still don't take me seriously," I said, disappointed.

"It's difficult. After all, you do have a tendency to contradict yourself."

I felt myself inflate before her, swell into the giant that I was. "My dear, Ms. Borgia," I said, offended. "I am a very learned man with vast knowledge. I hold two degrees from Fabian State, where I graduated with honors. Those contradictions that you accuse me of aren't really contradictions, but merely large thoughts that require more than fifty minutes to develop. If you bear with me, by the time the term is over and the last chapter of this great journey into world literature is completed, you will discover that I do have a cohesive message to deliver. You will then know from where I truly come."

"We'll see." She handed me a tract on the blessedness of humility. "I must go now, or I'll be late for my next class."

She then left the room like an honest-to-God woman, with enough swing to her hips to stop traffic on the interstate. The boys reacted immediately, when she reached the hall, and shouted her praises.

Now let's see what temptation does when our *Pippa passes!*

Once again Borlinda surprised us with her new look. Today it was her curly blonde hair, which fell heavily to her shoulders in doll-like abundance. Even her dress which complimented her superb body couldn't compete with all that hair. When she needed attention, which was frequently, she would pat or brush or finger it, and smile contentedly as the boys stared, fascinated. Since her private conversations with Erda, she had become very sensitive about her image and was always seeking the approval of her friends.

"Tell me the truth," I overheard her ask a male admirer. "Do I look like a good Christian girl? Or do I look cheap and available? Should I take it all to God in prayer? Or should I just conceal everything with less highlighting?"

"You must highlight your assets," I interrupted, eager to lead this good Christian girl to the Promise Land. "You must flaunt your virtues. Remember. It's for God's work." I gazed at her breasts which, even concealed, looked almost too big to be real. I then added: "So let everyone see how pure and unspoiled you are, so that we can all rejoice together."

She would then smile, pleased with my reaction, then hand me a tract. At such times, when she was generally satisfied with both her look and the compliments, she would usually remark in the voice of a philosopher uttering aphorisms: "God uses us in so many *wondrous* ways." Afterwards she would lift her mirror and gaze deeply at her reflection? For a 17-year-old girl, she certainly understood what being a woman was all about.

Her attractiveness wasn't just appreciated at school. Everyone who saw her immediately recognized it. When this Angel of God walked down the street, men turned and whistled. Even cars screeched to a stop, halting traffic. Eager to reach out and make new friends, she would approach the drivers and talk to them. But the conversations would abruptly end, with the men driving away quickly, when she started to read the Bible to them.

Thanks to all the attention she was receiving, she had little time left to irritate me. With her no longer a concern, I was free to concentrate on my main problem.

Unlike before, the students were no longer passive. In fact, because of all the vitamins they were taking, they were now sometimes *too* alert to teach. A speck of dust on their finger or a snow flake hitting the window was enough to distract them from what I was saying and cause them to exclaim with delight. To recapture their attention required me to use clever teaching strategies. Unfortunately, this only worked for brief intervals. With these seniors, I couldn't run with an idea (as I had with last year's seniors). They just refused to concentrate long enough to grasp the full significance of my thought. The exception was Roger. He was the only one who seemed to give full attention to whatever I said. This inability to hold the interest of the entire class disturbed me, because it was eroding my fine reputation as a teacher.

Consequently, I was obsessed with finding a way to reach them all. Until I had turned Borlinda into a free woman, and Pepe/Pepita had turned Niko into a eunuch, I would have to think of ways to interest my class without being controversial. Because of the enormous restrictions this caused academically, I was very worried about the effect of my continued failure on the education of my students. Then quite by accident I discovered a book at the grocery store which showed me how I could turn all my students into a Rhodes scholar without offending the sensibilities of the Borlindas or Nikos. The book was entitled simply *Into The Mind*.

Unlike most books on methodology, this one had many practical ideas. One which I particularly liked required a whirlpool design and an old motor. The motor, which the shop teacher gave me, was used to slowly turn the whirlpool design clockwise. After increasing the room temperature to 90 degrees, I shut off all the lights and pulled down the shades. I then turned on a spotlight, synchronized it to pulsate at a rate matching my brain waves, and aimed the pulsating light at the rotating whirlpool. In the background, to set the mood for my lecture, I played a tape of hymns, sung by a choir of castrated monks.

"Make yourself comfortable, and relax," I told the startled students who, while stripping themselves of layers of winter clothes, stared with amusement at the whirlpool. "That's it. Concentrate on the lovely design.

"Relax," I said, locking the classroom door to intruders. "Take a deep breath, and keep your eyes on the whirlpool— on the lovely design that flickers and turns before you. That's right. Relax and concentrate. Let the endless motion carry you off. Nothing else matters. Just my voice, that lovely design and those sweet angels singing."

"Awesome!" one student said, after swallowing a vitamin.

"Radical!" another student joined in.

Within minutes, every student was focused on the whirlpool, fascinated by its endless turning. I smiled victoriously. I felt like Julius Caesar before the Senate, announcing the defeat of Pharnaces. *Veni, vici, vidi.*

Successsss!

"That's right, relax! Let your body give in to the motion. Don't try to stop it. Just enjoy the journey, as you swirl and fall, weightless, out of control, deeper and deeper into space."

"Oh man!" one boy exclaimed, his eyes about to pop from their sockets from concentration. *"I'm flying!"*

"Relax," I continued. "Listen to the golden voices of those angels sing to you, beckoning you to Nirvana. Relax. Let yourself go. Deeper and deeper, and. . . ."

The room was silent except for the castrated monks who were singing like divas in unison. Every student was riveted to the whirlpool. When the entire class was mesmerized, staring ahead with bulging eyes, I shut off the monks and greedily ate several fat-free chocolate chip cookies, that Roger had left for me. Almost immediately upon finishing them, I felt a jolt, which caused my dentures to pop out.

Wow! I must get that recipe!

In the transcendental state that followed, I found myself filling with the wisdom of the ages. Today I was ready to set the foundation and provide the theme for all my lectures and tell them what I've only hinted at before. Today, I was going to free each and every student once and for all of their shallow existence by taking them to the edge of life, where I would inspire them to step into the universe and glimpse eternity. Today I was going to crack open their skulls and implant painlessly in their empty heads Truth, which I, their noble and capable teacher, knew well.

Like the aristocratic Englishman I was, I stood before them proudly, after devouring another cookie, and in a voice, which matched the gods, I began my lecture.

"All wisdom can be traced to three men, the triumvirate, as I prefer to call them," I said. "These three men in my opinion, and the opinion of anyone who really matters, have significantly effected history in ways no other men have or ever will."

(A very strange thing occurred, after eating the last cookie, I was no longer gazing ahead into the pulsating spotlight, observing stunned students studying a whirlpool. I was instead inside a kaleidoscope with colorful designs shifting and changing rapidly before me.)

"For those of you who have no mind," I said, continuing, "it may seem difficult to believe that the wisdom of three men could inspire significant historical change. But it's true. A good idea can change the course of history and lead the world from darkness to light. Such was the case in Greece about 400 B.C. There, a charming little Greek boy was born. His name was Plato. Unlike some of his contemporaries who grew up to be burly, gorilla types (like a certain staff member at Horace Mann), Plato instead resembled good English stock, lean, tall and elegant (like me, of course). What made him special was his remarkable understanding of life. From the very beginning, his ideas, especially on collectivism, have effected the course of history. Of course, scholars like me deserve some of the credit for that. By spreading Platonism, we have made it possible for the world to produce Qaddafis and Khomeinis."

(*Incredible!* Those colorful designs were beginning to whiz past me at supersonic speed. I must speak louder, so I can be heard above the sonic boom.)

"Remember, class," I said, raising my voice to its full resonance, "as one Frenchman once said. Oh what was that damn frog's name? Oh yes, Victor, Victor Hugo. As Hugo once said, nothing is mightier than an idea whose time has come. What was this idea that would change history—this idea whose time has *finally* come? Well, to put it simply, Plato discovered True Reality. 'What we see,' Plato had said, 'isn't reality, but only a fragment of it. True Reality exists beyond our perception, and it is nobler and greater than anything we can ever imagine.' Plato called True Reality the Ideal. I prefer to call it *Truth!*"

(*Extraordinary!* Not only can I hear those colorful designs in flight, but I can smell them as well. Why it's almost like burying my nose in my favorite bottle of *eau de cologne*.)

"Of course," I said, "it took another genius to tell us what we were waiting centuries to hear. It took Immanuel Kant to free us of those men, from Aristotle to Locke, who wanted us to use our brains. What did this clever little Kraut—I mean German—say? What was his brilliant discovery that so successfully brought a halt to the Age of Enlightenment?

"Well, it seems he discovered, not just one, but *two* realities! That's right, *two* realities! One is what we see and feel around us, and the other is what we can't see and feel, except, of course, by those like me who have a private hook up with Truth. But it took another Kraut—I mean, German— by the name of Georg Hegel, to show us the way to Truth through his clever philosophical observations.

"Some of you may ask: How does all this apply to us? How can we as mere students benefit from all this wisdom? How can we step to the edge of life and touch eternity? The answer is simple. The answer comes by enlarging your senses and enjoying what Shelley so poetically calls that 'Wild Spirit, which art moving everywhere.' It's as simple as that," I said, rejoicing in the elegance of my thought, "enlarge your senses, and step into the universe and let yourself be united with the great cosmic forces around you."

As I stared into the pulsating light show, enjoying a three-dimensional, Technicolor extravaganza, I experienced an extraordinary excitement. I found my spirit lift from my body like some ethereal facsimile of me, and soar like a rocket into space.

"Reason is dead," I said, as I took flight. "Thank you, my triumvirs, for freeing me. Without you, my three friends, I wouldn't be the liberated teacher I am. Without you, I would be tied to my limited perceptions, totally unfulfilled, and very much alone. Reason is dead," I cried out to the world below, as I flew toward heaven on a speck of light, "and I am free. . .*freeeee!*"

The following day, after returning from lunch, I saw a hand, clutching a Bible, rise above the heads of a group of boys. By the speed with which the Bible was moving, I knew Borlinda was in rare form. Eager to hear what she had to say, I hid behind a tree, beneath a branch where two squirrels were getting acquainted, and listened to this Child of God pour out her soul. I knew by the size of the audience and the sheer energy in her voice I would experience the results of all my efforts. I would see a new Borlinda, a woman totally realized, burst forth eagerly, ready to live. For the occasion, I removed my pocket tape recorder and began to tape the event for posterity.

She was standing on the school steps in her Levi's, sweater and unzipped leather jacket, resembling a Mona Lisa with a body of a Marilyn Monroe. There wasn't a boy in the crowd who wasn't enchanted, who wouldn't kill for a moment alone with her. When she spoke and thrust her Bible into the air, causing her breasts to leap forward, the crowd went wild, whistling and screaming with joy, at her wonderful display of religious fervor.

"It says right here," she said, waving the Bible in the air and swinging her breasts at the same time. "'Cursed be the man that trusteth in man, and maketh flesh his arm.' To do so shall be like a thorn in your side. But how many of you heed this? How many of you care?"

"Amen, sister," a boy shouted between puffs of an herbal cigarette he shared with friends. "*Amen!*"

Roger moved through the crowd. "Step right up, and get your afternoon vitamins," he said like a carnival barker. "Today's special, only two dollars each."

Borlinda glanced at him, one hand waving a Bible, the other on her hip. "Do you mind?" she asked, annoyed.

"I'll only be a minute," he said, quickly collecting money.

"Please hurry," she said, "or I'll strike you down with the Word of God."

Although she behaved as though she were disturbed by his interruption, I knew differently. After years of girl watching, I recognized her behavior as just an act, conceived to conceal her attraction. When he finished selling his pills and waved good-bye, she followed him with her gaze, as he disappeared into the school.

"Hey, Borlinda," someone shouted, popping a vitamin. "Remember us? We're the sinners you're trying to save!"

She turned to the crowd, embarrassed. "Of course. Where was I?"

"'Cursed be the man that trusteth in man,'" I shouted from my hiding place behind a tree.

"Thank you." She opened her Bible. "That's exactly what it says right here in Jeremiah 17:5. Yet how many of you heed the Word of God? If you did, you would never allow misguided teachers to lead you to your doom. Take that science teacher, for example. Who knows what might happen because of all that unsupervised experimenting she permits in class? There could be an explosion that could kill us all. But do you think she cares? Why should she? While you are carelessly mixing chemicals, she sits behind her desk reading pornographic love stories. But as derelict as she is in her duties, as dangerous as she is to your well-being, she is still a saint when compared to that *demented* lit teacher. What Mr. Hamme does. . . ."

At that point, my fascination turned to red-hot anger. *How dare that Polack call me demented.* I turned off the tape recorder, slipped into the building, then called the police.

"There's a girl at school breaking the law," I told the officer. "She's conducting a public rally without a permit."

I then marched to my classroom, and slammed the door behind me. That bitch is getting out of hand. Such gall. Who

does she think she is using a fine school like this to dissemi-
nate her Christian propaganda? *Demented?!* I'll show her
who's demented!

The newspaper office wasn't large, but it was private,
and not very far from my classroom. Sometimes after class I
would visit, just to enjoy the pleasure of being in the most
powerful room in the school, where ideas were put to words
and published for everyone to read.

No one but an editor knew how powerful the pen was. I
was standing by the window, gazing into the courtyard, pondering this when Roger entered. He approached me, not like
the descendant of a potato-picking Mick (as he once confessed), but like a proud, elegant Englishman of impeccable
breeding. How similar we were in style and character. Surely
he must be teasing me about his ancestry? Only born leaders presented themselves with such self-confidence.

"You wanted to talk?" he asked politely, after placing a
brown bag on the desk.

"Yes, Roger," I said, pleased to be with an equal. "You
know you've become quite popular since the publication of
your article. In fact, there's not a girl here who wouldn't
give up a year's allowance just to be alone with you."

"I know. They're becoming quite a nuisance."

"Well, I'm sure you have no trouble handling them."

"I don't exactly handle them. But I do sell them vitamins. I must admit that was a great idea of yours to run my
photo with the article. It's helped business tremendously."

"I have another idea, which you may also like."

"What's that?" he said.

"Well, there's a girl at school, Borlinda Borgia. . . ."

"You mean Miss Virgin Mary?"

"That's the one," I said. "You know she's quite anxious
to meet you."

"I know. She's always following me. Very strange girl."

"True, but a well-stacked, strange girl."

"Still, not my type."

"Why don't you pretend she is and loosen her up a little?"

"You're asking a lot, Frank."

"I could be very grateful."

He studied me from my well-cared-for head to my Gucci loafers, as though he were memorizing me. He then smiled. It was an attractive smile, a model's smile, all rosy cheeks and perfect white teeth.

"Then it's agreed?" I asked.

"Well, as I said, she isn't my type. But I do know someone at the club who might enjoy meeting her. He's always looking for new talent, and she just may be what he needs."

"You know, Roger," I said, pleased. "You've got to be English. No Mick—I mean, Irishman—would ever show such humanitarian concern for his fellowman."

"Of course, I would like a small favor in return."

"How much of a favor?"

"About 10 percent."

"Ten percent?"

"That's right. But I'll have to fill you in on the details later. Right now I've got to meet with my Jamaican supplier."

"What happened to your Colombian one?"

"He was killed at *La Esperanza*. But I met a new guy with fantastic connections who's teaching me how to make money by staying in school." He walked to the door. "See ya."

"Before you go," I said. "Could you leave me a cigarette?"

"Oh, Frank, I'm sorry. I just smoked the last one. But why don't you have one of those fat-free brownies I left for you on your desk. They're much better for you, and they should kill your craving for a smoke."

The brownie was good. It was thickly coated with a creamy chocolate frosting, and it immediately took my mind off cigarettes. As I ate it, my gaze drifted to the huge painting on the wall, which one of my students had given to me. The painting was a representation of the sun, which, even in the dark, lighted the room with its brilliant energy. It was remarkable how powerful this painting was, how simply it conveyed a great intellectual truth. By symbolically identifying the center of life as a ball of fire, the artist had reduced to one image what philosophers had dedicated books to.

The more I gazed at this painting, the more impressed I became of Mimi Flicop's talents. It was a pity she suddenly stopped painting. Her uncommissioned murals on office building walls, and her imaginative graffiti in department store bathrooms had made her quite famous.

Perhaps when she returns from this trip she was on she will paint again. Who knows what great ideas she will come back with? Who knows what new visions she will share with us after living on the edge of eternity for a while? How lucky she is. How wonderful it is for someone so young to be so free—to strip herself of her body and soar to heaven like a flash of light

I wonder how Mimi does it at will?

While staring at the painting, pondering its Great Truth—and eating another brownie—the image unexpectedly came alive for me. To my great surprise and pleasure, it suddenly exploded into one huge, red-hot flame, which began to turn on its axis.

As I watched the flame dance, sending its sparks flying, I felt myself dissolve from the intense heat as my soul rocketed on a white ray of light to the center of the flame.

What a genius! *WHAT A GENIUS!*

Pepe was in a rare mood today. He had his fingernails and toenails clipped and polished during lunch, and had just spent an exhausting morning trying on different wigs. Tonight he was going to have his show down with Niko Papalodopoulos, and he wanted to be certain that he had the right seductive look. His success with men depended on his ability to make them forget during the embrace that the she was really a he. Having fully developed breasts helped; having a smooth, almost baby-face complexion also helped. But what really made the difference were those lesson in being a lady he had gotten from the girls. As a result, he was convincing in either a bathing suit or a gown and could fool anyone, even me.

When Pepe was ready for a man, *he was a woman!*

"It's going to be a simple little meal, catered by the *Jeunesse Dorée Café,*" he told me privately in his office. "But it's going to be a nice meal. I want the aromas of good food to sharpen his senses. The rest Pepe/Pepita will do. Tonight it won't be a matter of which person I prefer. Tonight it's going to be which person *Niko* prefers."

"But what if he's not interested in either Pepe *or* Pepita?"

"Then I have no choice. To use your words, *I'll chop off his balls!*

Pleased with Niko's fate, I changed the subject to my other interest. "Incidentally, what's the latest on Borlinda's mother?"

"Didn't I tell you? She and Phyl have become bosom friends!"

"How does that bull. . .I mean, woman do it?"

"You underestimate Phyl, Frank. She's really a remarkable person. What I do to men, and you do to your students, she does to women. She is so good that several times she almost got into my pants! And you know how strict I am about that sort of thing. So it didn't surprise me to learn that Mrs. Borgia was no real challenge for her. In fact, the way Phyl tells it, it was really routine. The two of them just dropped to their knees and began praying for your soul. When they were through, Phyl served her some coffee—and those delicious fat-free brownies Roger sells—and the two spent the remaining afternoon getting all excited discussing fallen women in the Bible. I don't think Mrs. Borgia will ever be a problem again. Phyl is seeing to that by having her over regularly for prayer meetings and brownies."

"You two really impress me," I said in awe. "What you two are doing for humanity will be recorded in history."

Thanks to Roger Murphy, Borlinda was invited to her first dance at a popular downtown club. As a teacher committed to the full development of my students, I was most eager to observe Borlinda's coming out and, if necessary, guide it in the right direction with my infinite wisdom. For this momentous occasion, I decided to visit the club incognito. I didn't want to be identified if anything went wrong. Until she was permanently out of my life and safely enjoying hers, I had to be certain that my influence was invisible. After all, she might find some neurotic reason to disapprove. God only knows what that crazy bitch would do then. For her coming-out, I darkened my fair hair, then covered it with Vaseline for that greasy dago look. Afterwards, I put on a false mustache, a large distinctive Roman nose and tight black leather pants and shirt.

When I entered the club, I knew I could have my pick of anyone in sight. There wasn't one woman or man who didn't study me with interest. Because I wasn't there to dally, I decided to save my Italian gigolo look for another occasion when I was free to make new friends. So instead of talking to all the admiring strangers, I just leaned against a pillar and observed.

Many of the men and women, I noticed, looked very impressive in their high-fashion style. Some had their hair dyed orange, others purple, and still others green; a few went as far as to streak it with several colors. There were androgynies, clothed neither like men nor women, with spiked hairdos; chesty men with shoulder-length hair, wearing just bow ties and tight black pants; and New Wave models looking fragile and expensive in their *haute couture* and rainbow-painted faces.

In many cases, none of the clothes or colors matched. Some even clashed violently. But together they made a chic, *avant-garde* presentation, which was a delight to observe. It reminded me of a masquerade party, a fantasy, in which Truth was too abstract to grasp (except by those lucky few like me who could catch it all with one glimpse).

Several times I almost wanted to let myself go and enjoy the party. But I quickly stopped myself. Tonight I was here for another purpose.

A rap group called the Animals was performing in a cage suspended from the ceiling. They were gyrating to jungle sounds and talking quickly (sometimes even articulately about how it felt to be wild and caged). While they performed—one moment in complete darkness, the next moment in blinding light—the room exploded with images of wild animals stalking prey. Occasionally the dance floor would light up and the room would fill with smoke. As it did, images would dissolve into a thick, white cloud.

The music was loud, jungle-like, and deafening, and at first I had to cover my ears to protect them. But once I grew accustomed to the volume and had become deaf like everyone else, I was able to enjoy the spectacle without covering my ears. Fascinated by the sights, I began to realize how effective a light and sound show could be in a classroom. All I would need would be a slide projector, a few pulsating color spots, a smoke machine, and a stereo system. Within minutes, I could have my entire class pondering profundities.

Because of the visual confusion caused by the smoke and the light show, I was continuously distracted, and never certain of what I saw. (Was that boy masturbating or dancing? Was that girl holding a needle or a wine glass? Was that man sniffing or counting his money?)

Trying to sort this confusion became a challenge. For this reason, I didn't immediately see Borlinda standing directly in front of me, clinging to Roger. When I did notice her—during the period when the room briefly lighted up—she was so bewildered by what was happening around her that she didn't see Roger slip something into her soda. The next time I saw her she was no longer clinging to him. She was shaking her rear to the music like the others, which in her Levi's and sweater was quite a sight. If I didn't know who she was, I would have moved right in on her and would have given her a sample of perfection.

My ears were still ringing when the music ended, and it took a few minutes before I could hear again. En route to the bar, Borlinda stopped and stared at me. "Mr. Hamme, why are you dressed so funny?"

"My name *itsa* Luigi," I said with a thick Italian accent. "*Notta* Hamme."

"Well, whoever you are underneath all that grease and leather," she said, smiling innocently, "you sure look like my psychopathic English teacher."

Angered by her insolence, I gave her a famous Italian arm gesture. Then when she turned and walked away in disgust, I gave her another Italian gesture, right on her rear, sending her fleeing in terror into Roger's arms.

An exceptionally handsome young man approached Roger at the bar. The man had the sort of sensual maleness that could convert a nun into woman with just a smile.

"Okay," I overheard him say to Roger, "where is she?" Roger pointed to Borlinda who, after drinking another soda, was entertaining several men, shaking her hips without the accompaniment of music. "Not bad," he said, impressed. "Who is she? Some new student you are breaking in for your classmates?"

"Let's just say she's a friend I'm bringing out," Roger said.

"Suit yourself." He then removed a handful of large bills and gave several to Roger. "If she performs as well as she looks, she's going to make me one very rich man." He then approached Borlinda who immediately responded to his good looks, and she disappeared with him onto the dance floor. As I watched them vanish, I knew with a man like that as her instructor, she would be ready for the Olympics, when he was through.

I didn't see Borlinda for three days. Although I was curious and wanted to ask Roger about her, I didn't. I had too much to do, and I personally was delighted that she wasn't around to interrupt me.

I was in the newspaper office, editing the next issue of *The Inquisitor* when she unexpectedly entered. She was wearing the same clothes she wore at the club except, instead of now looking clean and pressed, they looked soiled and wrinkled. Her long blonde hair was uncombed and her sweater was inside out. Although I had remembered her breasts to be big, I had never remembered them to be *gigantic*. I was speechless when I saw her stagger toward me, somewhat dazed.

"Where have you been these past three days?"

She looked at me, confused. "Has it been three days?"

"You must've really had a good time."

"I think I did a movie, or did I watch a movie? Funny, nothing's clear."

"A movie?" I said.

"Oh yes, a religious epic. Something about this lovely Christian woman who's captured by these Roman soldiers and made to be their slave. In fact, Maurice. . . ."

"Who's Maurice?" I asked curiously.

"He's a movie producer friend of Roger's that I met at the club." She was swaying, looking very unsteady, as though any moment she might fall forward or backward. "Well,

Maurice said he wants to feature me in a series of Christian art film." She then slid her hand into her Levi's pocket and removed some big bills. "See, he gave me $500 for just reading the Bible—or was it Ovid? I just don't remember exactly. Anyway, he *loves* the way I read." She looked at me, bewildered. "Has it *really* been three days?"

I nodded.

"Strange," she said. "I don't remember being gone that long. Oh, well. I've got to go. Roger made an appointment for me to see Dr. Lee Linn this afternoon, and I just can't be late."

"Isn't he the plastic surgeon?" I said, surprised.

"Plastic surgeon? Oh, no. He's a G.P. Why would I see a plastic surgeon? Well, I've got to go now. I've only stopped by to tell you I won't be in class today."

She then left, bumping into the wall and nearly falling backwards onto her perfectly shaped ass. I smiled.

Thanks to temptation, that's going to be one less Angel of God to worry about!

Seven

After the *La Esperanza* incident, the IRS stepped up its crack down on foreigners who didn't pay their share of the taxes—and gunned them down in broad daylight! One day it was the Jamaicans, the next day the Colombians. It was shameful how these aliens would come here, earn good money, then expect to keep it all without sharing any of it with our Benevolent Uncle who made it all possible.

Fortunately, what happened in the city's business area didn't effect us at school. It only made us careful where we shopped. For Roger Murphy, the events created an opportunity to expand his market and sell his products at a larger profit.

As the neighborhood blazed with excitement, life continued at Horace Mann uneventfully. Then Jeremiah was murdered. According to eyewitness reports and the six o'clock news, Jeremiah was murdered in what was called gangland style.

Some of my students believed he was killed because of the article he was researching for *The Inquisitor*. These students feared, if they weren't careful of what they wrote, they would also end up like Jeremiah. I tried to calm them by reminding them that Jeremiah merely had the misfortune of being at the wrong place at the wrong time. But they didn't accept this explanation, claiming that he was sitting on his porch when shot.

While I began to explain to them the facts, I saw a note on my desk. It warned me that any future articles on drugs could result in my losing my brain to science. Amused, I dismissed the note as a student prank and, like the dedicated teacher I was, focused my attention on my staff's concerns.

"Some of you in your zeal for the big story think of us as a major daily," I told them. "Well, unfortunately, we aren't. We're merely a small student paper with limited staff and resources. For this reason, I think we must concentrate on what we do best. So let's leave the city news to the dailies and let's just cover the news at school that's fit to print."

The staff was delighted. One boy suggested we do something on the principal's strange behavior around the counselor, but I wisely objected and suggested they come up with an article idea that would be of more interest to their classmates.

"Then how about us interviewing students, and doing a piece entitled, 'My First Lay.'"

"Now that's more like it," I said approvingly. "But let's tone it down a little to avoid offending anyone and call it 'Cutting the Umbilical Cord With My First Kiss.'"

"I've got one," one girl shouted. "How about 'My Favorite High'?"

"Excellent! But don't forget to include those classroom lectures that made it possible."

"Hey, listen to this one!" one boy said. "Why don't we rate orgies? Maybe even have an orgy of the month column."

"Oh how original and imaginative," I said, impressed. "But let's call it party instead. Orgy is so negative."

When I told Pepe my decision, and showed him the note, he thought I had used good judgment. "We mustn't stick our nose into the affairs of the community. Our responsibility is to educate students, and what happens outside the school must be left to the proper authorities." He then showed me a note he had received. "If you continue to let that pornhead geek print any more issues on drugs, we're going to cut off your tits and hang them from the flag pole." He then told me that even Phyllis Jaffe had received a note.

"Her, too?" I said. "What did it say?"

"Something to the effect that if she continues to permit the schools to publish any more articles like those in *The Inquisition*, her virgin ass will be shipped to Colombia and used for recreation."

"Of course, we aren't going to be intimidated by them. Freedom of the press is at stake."

"You're absolutely right, Frank. That's why we will maintain a low profile on community affairs, at least until after the excitement passes."

"Exactly, Pepe. Afterwards, if the subject warrants it, we can do something scathing."

"Very sensible."

"Do you think this war in the streets will last long?"

"If it's anything like Latin countries, not more than a few weeks," Pepe said coolly. "After that, everything settles down again, until a new gang tries to take over. But meanwhile we must remember one thing."

"What's that?"

"We can't become too rigid in our point of view. We must be flexible, pragmatic, and move with the wind. . . ."

"You mean winners."

"The same thing."

Like the wise and dedicated teacher that I was, I decided to use the events in the community as the theme for my lecture. It was obvious by the students' preoccupation with Jeremiah's death that they now needed adult guidance to lead them out of their grief. For routine lectures, I would prepare them for what I had to say by simply reading to them several of my poems, which I filled with brilliant symbolism. ("I saw a crushed Coke can on the moon. In an alley a baby cried." Or: "While walking on the edge of time, a cow defecated in my path.") Once I had them pondering the meaning of such profound ideas and locked into some exact thought, I would then lead them into new areas of thinking. It was a clever technique I learned from reading *Into The Mind*. But today, because of the seriousness of the subject, I needed a swifter and more direct approach. So I removed the whirlpool design and pulsating spot, turned up the heat, then filled the room with the cries of castrated monks. After turning the students into bulging-eyed simians, I shut off the music and began my lecture.

"Beneath the veneer of civilization, the social and moral codes, the respectability," I said, "was the Unnatural Man. Who was this Man? What was he really like? In our history classes, we get a glimpse of him in the character of Thomas Jefferson and Benjamin Franklin. But it is in the novel *The Hunchback of Notre-Dame* that we truly get to know him. (*The Hunchback*, incidentally, is available at your favorite adult book store with John Holmes playing Captain Phoebus). For our discussion, I will talk about the movie version, rather than the novel, because the story is stronger. Simply stated, it is a story about Esmeralda and Captain Phoebus who meet and fall in love. But before they can consummate their love, Esmeralda is kidnapped by a grotesque hunchback named Quasimodo and held captive in a church bell tower where he tries to teach her to be honest and kind. Frightened by such unnatural behavior, Esmeralda kills the hunchback, then seeks refuge in the arms of Phoebus beneath a stained-glass window depicting the Transfiguration of Christ.

"Those of you concerned about the murders in the neighborhood wonder how this story is relevant to your experiences," I said. "Well, it's very simple. What you are seeing around you every day is the Esmeraldas in confrontation with the Quasimodos (the Unnatural Men in our society). As some of you may know, these Quasimodos are everywhere—in the churches, schools, and even in your homes. You can spot them easily, because they are always trying to retard you emotionally with all their don'ts. What you must do when you meet them is resist like Esmeralda and never yield to them. Remember. There is a greater force ahead ready to carry you upward on an escalator ride to the stars. To enjoy that ride to paradise, you must never allow the Quasimodos to get in the way of all those wild forces within you, screaming for release. So remember: live, live, *live!*"

As I spoke, I noticed Borlinda Borgia wasn't listening to me. Since her return from her three-day holiday, she was moody and restless, and proned to overreact. The slightest gesture of friendliness from the boys would be rejected with either a slap or a glare. By her attitude, I knew she needed to be loosened up again. So I stepped in front of her and gave her a full view of my glory.

With legs and arms outstretched, head titled upward, as though speaking to God, I filled the room with profundities even Nietzsche would have difficulty matching. After she had an opportunity to enjoy my new scent (and a close-up of my male splendor), I returned to my desk and observed its effect on her. Instead of turning her into an eager woman, ready to devour life, as I had hoped, she covered her mouth and nose as if she were gagging and ran from the room.

I give up on that girl. Absolutely give up.

A change occurred, after my incisive lecture on the triumvirs and the Unnatural Man. All barriers between me and my students disappeared, and we became one. My students would surprise me by asking me brilliant questions. (Why is Medea a good role model for expecting mothers? Or: When

Voltaire suggested in *Candide* that we should cultivate our garden, what natural herbs did he recommend for us to grow? Or: Besides that memorable quotation in 'Ode on A Grecian Urn'—"Heard melodies are sweet, but unheard melodies are sweeter"—what other important recommendations for dealing with the underprivileged did Keats make in his poems?)

I actually enjoyed talking with the students and sharing ideas with them, because they began to grasp the significance of my message. Of course, there were a few who couldn't be reached, primarily because of health problems. But there were always those in every class. I could always spot them. They had that burned-out, zombie-like look of someone totally spent, who moved about the school with a glazed, dull stare. When they attended class, they were always coughing. Sometimes I would see them in the hall, vomiting. But again this was only a small fraction (about 25 percent of the class). For classes as large as mine, such a percentage was expected.

The majority seemed alive, full of energy (thanks to all the vitamins they took), and even ethnically aware (thanks to my respect for different cultures). I was glad to see they were finally behaving like teenagers and enjoying an occasional difference of opinion. Of course, it did upset me to learn that one student got his nose broken and another got stabbed during a disagreement. But then kids will be kids. The important thing is that they were becoming serious and forming strong opinions. Yes, I was very proud of what was happening at Horace Mann and pleased by my contribution to it.

I often wondered what sort of teacher I would be today, if I had teachers like me to guide me during my formative years. I was reminded of some of my teachers. Next to my special talents, they were amateurs. Yet they still managed to prepare me for this moment. It was their unique voice, though not as strong as mine, that made me the special teacher that I am today.

At such times, I would be reminded of one of my professors, whom I loved dearly, because he told me something that to this day I have not forgotten. He believed, and wisely, that a teacher ought to make his subject obtuse. The good students, because of their great minds, would have little difficulty comprehending what you meant, while the rest would be forced to come to you for assistance.

I have always appreciated such wisdom, shared with me during our after-class conversations. Although some of this information was not germane to what we were studying, it was always relevant to my interests. Consequently, it generated an enthusiasm for the subject that often lasted for the duration of our discussion.

But my real learning took place in those few classes where all traditional academic barriers were dropped, and the professors would encourage original research on any subject of my choice. It was in these classes that I began to form some of my new ideas, which have since become so important to my teaching style.

Two papers that I had done for these profs became the talk of the university. ("Involuntary Conjugation among Eighteen Century Turk Essayists," and "Spontaneous Heads and Tails Rhythms in French and Greek Poetry.") These papers confirmed my position as a first-class scholar and opened new opportunities for me on campus. After that, it was easy to convince some of my other professors of the need for me to replace the authors on their reading lists with popular writers of my choice. Some even agreed, as I so deeply believe, that the classics, to appeal to contemporary tastes, required a fresh approach, which only modern writers were courageous enough to offer. Those rare professors who had the nerve to disagree were quickly labeled for what they were, anti-egalitarians and fascists, and through my stu-

dent pressure, encouraged to be more sensitive to my twen-
tieth-century interests.

Fortunately, most of my professors recognized my special academic talent, and they made an effort to appeal to
my tastes. Some adjusted their lectures to accommodate me,
others even learned from me. One professor, who had me
read a novel a week, was so impressed after four weeks with
my ability to grasp subtle symbolism in literature that he
gave me an A, then dismissed me from class. Another professor (a linguistic analyst) confessed to me, after I presented
a brilliant report on comic-book classics, that being cultured
was elitist: "To expect too much from students can deprive
them of democracy, which needs a comic-book mentality to
appreciate. But even more important, it can undermine the
self-esteem of those who can't achieve reasonable standards."

Another professor, after reading my research paper, congratulated me on my observation that words meant nothing, that a story or a poem was merely sound without meaning. In praise, he wrote a brilliant book documenting this
point and dedicated it to me. The acceptance of this idea by
both critics and colleagues immediately opened the door for
all types of new and exciting research for me. Thanks to these
special educators, I was allowed to blossom and head the
new intelligentsia. Of course, because of my specialized education, I had little shared interest with the majority at college, except on such subjects as the football (which I rarely
watched) or the recent party (which I never attended).

As I reflected over my education, I became impressed
with all the useful knowledge I had accumulated. Whenever
I find myself expounding sagaciously in class, I am reminded
of all my courageous teachers who over the years have made
this moment possible by allowing me to be myself.

Each semester I volunteered for cafeteria duty, because
it gave me the opportunity to observe how the seniors spent

their time. But most of all, it provided me with the data to evaluate the results of my lessons. It always amazed me how significantly the seniors changed, usually in just a few short months, because of my inspiration.

At the beginning of the term, the only time you saw boys and girls together was when a few precocious girls decided to dazzle a group of boys with their feminine charm and spontaneous wit. But as the term progressed (largely due to the encouragement of devoted teachers like me and, of course, Erda Von Schwantz), there was a healthier contact between the sexes, a more natural mix of boys and girls.

This term it all started when someone introduced a party game called spin the bottle. The lucky pair matched by this game would disappear under the table and discretely kiss. Sometimes the kissing would get out of hand, and I'd see clothes fly into the air. But I never interfered unless the cheering and shouting got too wild and disturbed the others. At such times, I would blow my silver whistle, worn chained to my neck, and remind them to control their excitement.

Most of my students, like the spin-the-bottle enthusiasts, required minimal reminding. This was also true of those students with headset radios. These music lovers (head-bangers, as the kids called them) would sit quietly in their seats, shaking their bodies to the music, as they listened to every note and musical nuance at full blast! Perhaps some day because of this passion for music (that I fully encouraged), one of them would become another Chopin or Mozart.

Very little of the cafeteria food was ever eaten. Many students maintained their energy by buying everything from fat-free brownies to vitamin pills from a group of boys who worked for Roger Murphy. Permitting Roger to sell his vitamins and health food in the cafeteria (for a *mere* 10 percent of the profits) was my way of thanking him for taking such a special interest in Borlinda. From the first day, his business was a success. Sometimes in their eagerness to make a purchase, the kids would become disorderly. This would occasionally lead to a little shoving and pushing, and fist swinging. When this occurred, I would remind them of my disapproval by blowing my whistle, and immediately they would behave. This simple warning, reinforced by a little assistance from several football players, was usually all that was necessary to end the disorder and to get them to buy their health items in a civilized manner.

Occasionally a student would smoke one of those pleasantly aromatic herbal cigarettes, which I liked so much, and I would have to ask him to finish it outside, because the health department regulations strictly forbade smoking in the lunch room. But for the most part, the boys and girls understood the rules, which were few and reasonable, and they behaved in a manner that made me, as their Renaissance teacher, very proud of them.

The only time this wasn't the case was when a student would occasionally become sick and would have to be taken home. At such times, the dietitian would blame me for allowing the "student vendors" to sell all that junk, and I in retaliation would blame her for serving all that undercooked and tainted food that her staff prepared. Usually a truce would be reached before the battle became heated (thanks to Roger's private conversations with her) and both sides would agree that the unexpected illnesses were undoubtedly caused by the flu.

In general, it pleased me when things worked out. What happened here, when students were free to be themselves, reflected on every teacher at Horace Mann. Seeing all those happy kids enjoy themselves made me realize there was by far too much negative press on the public schools. Few parents realized the great job teachers like me were doing daily. Many didn't know about our many sacrifices to teach, the long hours we worked for a pittance. They just accepted the negative news reports as true without considering the fact that maybe the media was wrong, maybe there were many fine schools like Horace Mann that deserved our accolades.

One day I will tell parents this, one day I will confirm to the world that Horace Mann exists and is doing a noble job at educating Americans!

As I pondered our academic successes, while moving about the cafeteria, gently reminding students not to jump from the tables or to throw food at each other, I was suddenly startled by what sounded like firecrackers exploding. When I turned, several men were fleeing from the cafeteria. On the floor, lying motionless leaking blood, were the two vitamin-pill vendors.

I was stunned by what I saw. The idea of violence at Horace Mann was unbelievable. Quickly I overcame my shock and responded to the emergency in the professional manner expected of a public school teacher. I pushed my way through the crowd of students who were grabbing brownies, pills and cigarettes, spilling from the vendors' bags, and removed a note pinned to a victim's shirt ("Let this be a warning, gringo! Peddle your pills elsewhere.") and the ten twenty-dollar bills, clutched in the other victim's hand, before calling the police. The two-carat diamond ring that the other victim wore was impossible to remove, so I reluctantly left that for someone else. I gave the note to Pepe, and kept the money for my favorite charity.

The police treated the deaths routinely and interrogated me, a few students, and the cafeteria help. Since no one knew anything, and all we could tell them was what we suspected, the police had little to go on. After all, the facts were all quite obvious. Two students, running a little business with teacher approval, were robbed and killed by several rough men (obviously druggies from off the street looking for quick money for their habit).

When the television crew arrived for an interview, I revealed my most attractive look, exposed a little more chest hair than usual, and proceeded to give the reporter a summary of life at Horace Mann High during lunch hour. The reporter, uninterested in daily life at school, wanted to discuss international issues. "There are rumors of a war in the neighborhood between the Jamaicans and Colombians for the lucrative drug trade. Were these two boys part of it?"

"Tom and Dick were two fine students who were dedicated to European studies. The last thing these two pure-blooded Anglo-Saxons were interested in was Latin American problems."

"Well, if that's true and they aren't working for the Jamaicans, then how do you explain their recent cash purchase of a BMW?"

"I understand they come from wealthy families."

"According to the Department of Social Services, Tom's mother is on welfare and Dick's father was killed in a bank robbery last year. How do you explain that?"

I was genuinely confused. "Obviously someone's facts are wrong."

"That's our conclusion also. Thank you, Mr. Hammy."

"The 'E' is silent," I said politely.

Pepe was very upset about the cafeteria incident and all the phone calls from angry parents that would follow once the news broke. To resolve this matter before it became public, he contacted Phyllis Jaffe, who called Senator Waters, who contacted the President of the United States. As suddenly as the incident had occurred, it was over. The television interview was never aired, and the police reported finding the bodies in an alley five blocks from the school. There was no mention made of the diamond ring. According to the news report, the students were robbed during a holdup and stripped of their possessions by an unidentified assailant. One finger had been mysteriously mutilated, then discarded near the scene of the crime. Students who had seen what had happened in the cafeteria came down with a bad case of laryngitis and were unable to talk to anyone for several weeks.

"I'm pleased we ended this matter so favorably," Pepe said confidentially. "Just a breath of scandal, linking our school with some street gang, could tarnish our image. As you know that could be embarrassing for the President, who has always been such a strong supporter of our Renaissance school. So to avoid any possible reoccurrence, from this moment on, Phyllis absolutely forbids any business enterprise to exist on school property. Please tell your students that immediately."

"But don't you think that's overreacting a little?" I asked.

"No more businesses, Frank. None. *Nada!* Understand?"

I nodded, thinking of that extra money, which I would never earn again, and left his office, saddened by his unreasonableness.

Roger solved the problem it created by selling his vitamins in front of the school from a van. Since his business enterprise wasn't on school grounds, and since Pepe insisted that we shouldn't concern ourselves with what went on off-campus, it never became an issue. I did the sensible thing. When kids were late for class, after making a curbside purchase, I simply ignored it. For my consideration, Roger saw to it that I continued to receive a small weekly cash donation.

Shortly after the cafeteria incident, there was an increase of murder in the neighborhood. Alarmed by the unexpected rise, Pepe and I held a private meeting on the subject. During our discussion, the science teacher burst into the office.

"You'll never believe what happened," she said hysterically. "It was horrible—the guns, the blood. Oh Pepe, what's this world coming to?"

"What are you talking about, Takeshi?" Pepe asked.

"I'm talking about murder, Pepe. *Murder*."

"Not at school again!" Pepe said, horrified, springing to his feet.

"No, no, no, not here."

"Oh good," he said, relieved. "For a moment, you had me worried."

"But it was *horrible*, Pepe—one of the most horrible things I've ever seen!"

"I'm sure it was, my dear." He removed his Valium from the drawer. "Here, have a couple. Sorry I don't have any brandy to take with it."

She swallowed the pill with some water.

"Now tell me, Takeshi, *calmly*, what happened?" I asked curiously.

"Well, I was in this drug store on Market Street . . ."

"On Market Street? Oh, Takeshi, what am I going to do with you?" Pepe said. "Didn't I warn everyone in my memo to avoid that area?"

"I know, but I needed a new romance novel to read, and I didn't think it would be a problem to buy one there during lunch hour." She began to cry. "Then it happened."

"What happened?" I asked impatiently.

"This black Jaguar pulls up and two masked men start shooting at several pedestrians standing outside, talking. It was awful. There I was in the drug store looking out the window right at these masked killers, and one of them just stared at me before they drove away. I don't know what he was thinking. But something about him reminded me of one of our students."

"One of our students?" I said, shocked. "Surely you jest," I said. "None of our students would do a thing like that!"

"I must go to the police. I could never live with myself if I didn't go to the police and tell them everything."

Pepe became nervous suddenly. "You mustn't act hastily," Pepe said cautiously. "Remember, you could be wrong and, in the process, damage the school's reputation. So why don't you think about it before you act, and we can talk about it later." Then he quickly changed the subject and talked about the great new concept in education, being advanced here, which, when duplicated throughout America as the President planned, would reverse the decline of modern education. The young teacher listened tolerantly for a few minutes, then grew anxious.

"I've got to go to the police," she interrupted suddenly. "I just don't think I could face myself if I didn't."

"Let me call Phyllis," Pepe said, trying to calm her, "and see what she suggests. I'll get right back with you, I promise." The teacher thanked Pepe and, after she left, he turned to me and said: "Being a principal, Frank, sometimes can be a real bitch!"

Takeshi was never seen by us again alive. That afternoon she was hit by a car while walking home from school. The car was traveling along the sidewalk at fifty miles an hour in a twenty-five-mile-an-hour school zone. Of course, no one was able to identify the car. It was just one of those black, expensive-looking foreign cars.

Two days later Pepe hired a new science teacher. During the faculty meeting, after a lengthy talk about our school's noble dedication to learning, he introduced the man.

"Takeshi," Pepe said, "was an excellent teacher, and we are all saddened by her death. Her unusual commitment to teaching and her deep love for her students will always be remembered. Finding a replacement for her wasn't easy. It required me to search high and low to locate someone with her impeccable background and skill. Such a teacher I think I've found in Ollie Olson. Mr. Olson who has a Master's in modern dance has taught science for ten years at Skylark State Penitentiary. Because of his excellent background, we all should learn a great deal from him. So please say hello to him and let him thrill you (as he had me) with his interesting observations about life behind bars."

Everyone immediately liked Ollie, because he provided us with a fresh view of life. Overnight the students revealed an interest in science, which impressed even Ollie, and they filled his classes to the brim. Many cut other classes (including mine!) just for a chance to stand against the wall and to hear him speak. Because of his remarkable success, I asked for permission to sit in on a class and learn firsthand from him his teaching technique. He, of course, was delighted to accommodate me, and flattered that someone with my reputation was interested in learning from him. From the very moment I heard him speak, I understood why he was so popular. He did exactly what all good teachers have been doing for millenniums: *He made his lessons relevant!*

"Teaching at the state pen taught me a great deal," he began. "I learned things from those guys that will remain with me all my life. Many of those men sent up would still be outside making it, if they had mastered what I call the Three Golden Rules for Survival. But they were small-time thugs with good ideas, and no *savoir faire*. You got to have *savoir faire,* if you are going to make it in the world of scientific research. Me, I'm a science teacher, and I get my kicks from sharing with you my formulas. But some of you may someday want to become big-time scientists, and if you want to survive well, you're going to need to know more than a few formulas. You're going to have to know the Three Golden Rules.

"The first one, and a very important first one at that, is: *grease hands!* Remember that, and life will reward you generously. But greasing hands isn't all. If you really want to make it big (and remain big) you're going to have to learn Golden Rule Two.

"Golden Rule Two simply says: *build an empire!* This you do by creating a research laboratory and a network in which others work for you. Remember: You can't do everything yourself. You need help. But also remember, you are only as good as those working for you. So be sure of those you hire. Real success only comes to those who build an efficient and *silent* family! This is especially important in the cut-throat, competitive world of scientific research.

"And finally, we come to Golden Rule Three: *maintain security.* This is very important if you want to protect your research during a crisis. To do this you must make certain no one knows who is doing what for whom."

Within a short time after Ollie's arrival, the street wars ended. Roger Murphy, who became one of Ollie's most devoted science students, began to apply his ideas to the vitamin pill business.

Eight

Pepe flew into the faculty meeting, his hands waving, his breasts bouncing. He looked like a disheveled cross-dresser who had just been raped with his/her clothes on.

"Wait 'till you hear the news," he said in a voice a little too high for Pepe, though in the perfect pitch for Pepita. All conversation stopped, and everyone turned to hear the Latin bombshell transvestite speak. "Thanks to the President of the United States' wife, Horace Mann High has been awarded a special teaching grant!"

I immediately sat up, alert, smiling. Life always seemed brighter when money was discussed. I wondered how much was involved and what one needed to do to get it.

"As you know," Pepe began, "the President of the United States is monitoring our school. He is very much interested in what we do, because he wants to use our school as a model for other American schools. So it's essential that we always do our best and be as innovative as possible. I can't stress enough how important this is to the general success of the public schools. For some peculiar reason, which eludes me totally, the public doesn't have any trust in our schools. Many believe you teachers are overpaid underachievers and our schools are a multi-billion-dollar racket (as one so-called critic proclaims). Well, of course, we know differently. We know that Horace Mann High is the best damn school in the country with the *best* students, the *best* teachers and the *best* curriculum!"

Will he ever get to the point? Sometimes he can be maddening the way he beats around the bush. I better stop him before he drives us all crazy saying nothing.

"Pepe," I said. "Regarding the teaching grant, does that mean more money for us?"

"Be patient, Frank," he said. "Let me explain so there won't be any misunderstandings."

For the next ten minutes he talked about the Renaissance school, the important social and educational service it was providing. He explained how the President was planning to trim Social Security and the Medicare benefits so more money could be made available for bigger and better schools just like ours. "Education, my dear friends and colleagues, is the single most important program our government sponsors. Our success at teaching will not only determine the future of American children, but it will also determine the quality of life for all of us tomorrow. Never forget. These children will be our leaders some day and will provide us with the services that we in our golden years will depend upon for our survival."

Get to the point. Damn it. *HOW MUCH MONEY IS THERE?*

"Tonight on television the President will explain his plan for the American public schools, his *new* plan in which our school will be used as his model to help him win financial support from the public for long-needed education reform. From what the superintendent told me over lunch today at *La Cage aux Folles,* his wife deserves all the credit for his plan. It seems she came up with the idea while eating chocolate, raspberry cake. Rumors are the President always gives her a slice whenever he needs solutions to vexing problems. (I'll never understand how she ever maintains such a great figure eating so much cake.) Anyway, while eating cake last night (with homemade whipped cream on it, mind you!), she got this great idea for getting kids more involved in their education. I understand she first tested the idea during her lean years, when her husband was just another struggling senator, seeking handouts in Washington. As you may have read in the press, she was once a substitute teacher who supplemented her husband's meager six-figure income teaching the underprivileged in Chevy Chase, Maryland."

My God, is he ever going to get to the point? Who gives a damn about the President's wife?

"Although her idea for revolutionizing education isn't particularly new, it is still bold and brilliant, if I may say so myself. Simply stated the plan is this: The President wants us to enlarge our students' experience by turning over some of the teaching to them. That means each of you will select a student to teach one of your classes, and you will grade this student on how well he succeeds. To motivate them, each student chosen will be paid $50 a week."

"Pepe," one teacher interrupted. "Do you think that's wise? Many kids can't even read. How will they ever teach, if they can't read?"

"Teaching," Pepe said, "as we all know, is a challenge that demands the highest level of dedication. We mustn't allow ourselves to be discouraged by such negatives. Besides, we aren't expecting them to learn *new* information. We merely want to hear what they already know. So let them talk. Let their thoughts flow. That's all he expects. That's all any of us can expect."

"What about us?" I said, thinking how inadequate my $45,000 a year salary was for meeting payments on my car and condo. "How much is there for *us*, Pepe?"

"I was just getting to that, Frank. You really must learn to be more patient," Pepe said. "Now as Frank so eagerly wants to know, what does this all mean in dollars and cents for you? Well, for a start the school will receive a flat award of $25,000, which can be spent however we choose. I thought, since we have all worked so hard that we should spend some of that money on a fabulous costume ball at the Cotillion Room of Edmund Park Hotel. We can come dressed as our favorite movie star. Won't that be such fun?"

Doesn't that drag queen think of anything else? The money, Pepe. For God's sake, *HOW MUCH MONEY?*

"Oh yes, what was I saying?"

"The money, Pepe," I said.

"Thank you, Frank," Pepe said. "Of course, I am sure all of you want to know how much you'll each get. Well, you must remember that we are educators and, for us as educators, there is never enough money available to reward us properly for all our great sacrifices and efforts. The President realizes this, and he regrets that he can't be more generous. All he can give you for this additional responsibility is an extra $300 per paycheck, or $5,400 a year. Now I know that isn't much money. I spent more than that annually on my evening clothes. But you must look at the brighter side. You'll not only have one less class to teach each week, but you will also have the thrill of watching your students grow intellectually. As I mentioned, his wife had whipped cream on her cake. So she felt especially generous. That's why she recommended this year's Teacher of the Year award goes to the teacher who successfully turns a student onto teaching. The lucky teacher will enjoy radio, television and newspaper coverage, receive a $10,000 tax-free bonus, and be invited to write an article for *The American Public School Journal for the Affirmation of Pedagogic Integrity.*"

The American Public School Journal, $10,000, radio, television, and newspaper coverage. Now we're talking perks! I must remember to send the President's wife a ten-pound Sacher Torte.

"Are there any questions?"

"Yes, when do we start?" I said enthusiastically.

"I knew I could count on your support, Frank," Pepe said. "In answer to your question, right away. Now who'd like to be on the planning committee for the costume ball?"

The following day I discussed the student-teacher program with the class. I told them what a great opportunity it was for the lucky student chosen, and I reiterated some of the points that Pepe made.

"Education, my dear students," I began, "is the single most important program our government sponsors. What happens in the classroom today directly effects our quality of life tomorrow."

"What the hell are you talking about?" one boy said.

"I said that education is the single most important. . . ."

"Yeah, yeah I got that. Get to the point."

I looked at him, annoyed. It was impossible to expound sagaciously if students needed everything reduced to the simple. Rather than resist, I yielded and said: "Who would like to earn $50 a week teaching a lit class?"

He sneered. "Are you kidding?" he said. "That doesn't even cover a day's smokes!"

His crass materialism shocked me. I couldn't believe that one of my students whom I was so carefully nurturing to appreciate great ideas would think like that. "You can't put dollars and cents on this type of experience," I said, revealing my disappointment. "You must think of it as an opportunity to teach young minds, and do something important with your life."

"Hey, man. Fifty bucks. Get real. My sister makes twice that an hour hustling Jews."

I must make a note to get to know that boy a little better. One hundred dollars an hour. Not bad for a young career girl. Maybe I could moonlight.

"You know, Mr. Hamme," Roger said, suddenly rising. "I agree with you. It isn't the money. It's the opportunity to do a social good, and if you will be kind enough to consider me, I would really appreciate it."

"Who's he trying to bull," one student responded.

"Yeah," a girl sneered. "Get him!"

I ignored their reaction and used the moment to lead thought in a new direction. "I am very pleased with your altruistic attitude, Roger," I began. "Sometimes in life we are called upon to make certain sacrifices for the general good. As a teacher dedicated to. . . ."

The students knew by my tone that I was about to fill the room with profundities. Some began to rest their heads on the desk in a listening position, while others, after popping a vitamin, slouched in their chairs and gazed at me with dazed awe. Seeing them so ready for serious thought made me realize how significantly I had changed them in such a short time.

I was pleased that Roger Murphy wanted to teach. He was exactly the type needed in the profession. There were by far too many powder puffs and so few real men. What the profession needed were positive leaders to guide kids to their intellectual summit. Under my able direction, I had no doubts that Roger would become such a leader.

Who would have ever guessed that this young Apollo, who held the world exactly where every red-blooded American boy should, would want to dedicate his life, not to frivolity, but to teaching others. I would never have thought that he would make such a decision, especially when he was doing so well selling vitamins. I guess in my special way, through the magic of my teaching, I had inspired him to do more with his life than just sell pills.

What a victory for me. How special it makes me feel. There's just no limit to what I can do when I set my mind to it. Maybe now that he will be helping me with my teaching,

I can help him sell pills. Selling vitamins shouldn't be very difficult, especially for someone as verbally dexterous as I, and it's so profitable. I'm sure I can not only run his business successfully part-time, but also double his profits. Any business that provides a boy with enough money to buy a Jaguar and a dime-size-diamond earring for his right ear is one I should certainly take seriously.

"Your desire to teach impresses me," I told Roger privately. "Here you are at an age when a young man's fancy turns to thoughts of girls. . . ."

"Frank," he interrupted, smiling, "there are other things besides girls."

He then winked at me. I assumed by his winking he thought I understood, but I was confused. Next to girls, for a healthy boy like Roger, what else is there?

"Money?" I asked uncertainly.

He laughed. "No, not money either." And his gaze made a tour of me that was quite flattering, but confusing because I didn't look my best at the end of the day. My manly face needed shaving, my disobedient cowlick broke free of the hair cream, and my designer clothes resembled a table cloth after a banquet. But then I was obviously being too hard on me. I often forget that even in my after-three look, I can still be quite a thrill. I guess I'm so spoiled by my dazzling beauty, when I'm at my best, that I don't appreciate how stunning I still am after five hours of teaching.

"Well, whatever it is, I'm glad you decided to teach."

"Did anyone ever tell you you had beautiful buns?" he said unexpectedly.

"Beautiful buns?" I turned my head and tried to catch a glimpse of them, but, without a mirror, couldn't. I had to rely on my memory, which confirmed his observation. Many times standing by the mirror, I would say exactly that. In fact, I had always thought they were exceptionally firm and full, and in the right pants with the right cut, a pleasure to view. I smiled, pleased by the compliment. "That's kind of you to notice."

"There are lots of things about you I notice."

"Now that we will be working together, you must tell me everything."

"I'll do that," he said. Again he winked, and again I was confused. Maybe he wasn't trying to say anything to me. Maybe he just had something in his eye. Regardless, I was pleased to have such a polite and observant assistant as Roger. I was certain together we would bring new insight to literature.

When I entered the teachers' lounge, the teachers were discussing the President's wife's decision. I located a vacant chair near a group around a table. They were sharing a large pepperoni pizza. I was about to help myself to the last piece, when a teacher unexpectedly grabbed it, leaving me only with a pepperoni that had fallen from it. I picked up the pepperoni and ate it, then watched the others eat their slice.

"Do you realize I didn't get one volunteer? I actually had to beg a student to accept the teaching job, and she only agreed if I prepared the lessons."

"What are you complaining about? None of us had better luck."

"That's where you're wrong," another teacher said. "I heard the science teacher was deluged with offers?"

"The science teacher?" I said, puzzled. "Why should he have better response than the rest of us? Everyone knows science only deals with reality, while literature, really *great* literature, deals with the supernatural!"

"You know what I think?" another teacher said, ignoring my remark. "I think the President's wife should stop eating chocolate, raspberry cake."

"Can you believe that woman?" someone else responded. "Some twenty-five years ago she substitutes in a swanky suburb for a year or two, and she thinks she knows what needs to be done in our schools today. I have been teaching for ten years, and I don't even presume to know that."

I remembered a news report of the President and his family celebrating Thanksgiving at their mountain retreat, all smiles and hugs. "Some people have insight into teaching," I said in defense of the first family, "because of their success as parents."

"Some insight," another teacher laughed, "the boy is a head and the girl is a nympho!"

"I think the media has been very hard on the kids. After all, they're only normal teenagers sowing a few wild oats."

The math teacher stared at me strangely. I wondered if it were because of that pimple on my cheek, which I had squeezed earlier. Maybe I should have covered the bruise with makeup.

"Personally," another teacher said, "I don't think it matters who teaches. It's all the same, despite whether it's an Einstein or a chimp. They still learn nothing. So why not let the ignorant lecture the ignorant? Watching the performance should provide some good laughs."

"I think you are mistaken," I said. "Laughs aren't what we will get, but culture being passed from one generation to another. To quote John Dewey, 'schools should present life as real and vital to the child as that which he knows in the home, in the neighborhood, or on the playground.' What would be a better way to do this than to let students instruct us about *their* world."

Again the math teacher stared at me strangely. I really must make it a point, after squeezing pimples, to hide the blemishes with makeup.

"Zahida's right. It should give us a few good laughs," one teacher said. "I tried it during first-period history, and I found it hilarious."

"What happened?" another teacher asked.

"Well, it seems my student teacher had the impression that the first Early American Colonies were in Brazil. If she continues to think like that, can you imagine how she'll do on her SAT?"

"Brazil?" one teacher said, laughing. "You've got to be kidding?"

Confused by her amusement, I decided to interrupt the conversation and defend the young student. "Personally I think she's brilliant," I said to the startled listeners. "If she continues to show that type of precocity, she ought to do quite well on the SAT. Dr. Ching at Fabian State said something similar in his book, *South of the Border*. His thesis in this new look at early Americana was that Columbus didn't discover the West Indies but Brazil."

At that point everyone left, except the math teacher. She turned her chair toward me, tucked at her skirt a little to cover her lovely knee caps and, in a ladylike way, smiled just enough to reveal her utter fascination with my strong, male presence. "You can't imagine how deeply you interest me," she said. "Your views, they're so. . .well, fascinating. Where did you *ever* go to school?"

I immediately liked her. She was obviously a woman who understood that the quickest way to a man's heart was to get him to talk about himself! So many women forget this and just chatter endlessly about themselves. But this young lady was different, wiser. She recognized superior knowledge. For that reason, I felt it was my duty to tell her everything.

"Unlike most people," I said, recounting my early education, "I wasn't quite so lucky in the beginning. My first six months I spent in a private school in the Midwest. Unfortunately, the program there wasn't acceptable academically. There was by far too much reading and writing, and not enough fun and games. My parents had to remove me, after I cracked a teacher's skull with a paperweight, when she had the nerve to interrupt one of my classroom fist fights. Because of this incident, I had to spend the next six months on a sofa, talking to a man in white. After getting to know me and learning about my academic aspirations, he recommended to my parents, because of my special talents, that I should be placed in the public schools. Of course, the man was quite correct. The moment I entered Roosevelt Elementary and saw all those happy children running and playing and throwing things, I felt immediately at home. My first grade teacher was so fascinated with my precocity and quick adjustment that she double-promoted me!

"In fact, from the very beginning most of my teachers were impressed with my sophisticated knowledge. While the other kids were struggling to catch up with me, I was allowed to spend my day at the lavatory blowing smoke rings or wandering the halls spray-painting profundities on the walls. Thanks to my basic intelligence—and the skill of a reading teacher—by the time I was ready to graduate from eighth grade I had memorized enough words to read a primer all by myself. My parents were so proud of this achievement that they again enrolled me in a private school. Like before, the school program wasn't suited for my budding genius. There was too much history, math, science, and English, and none of those really important basics like 'Primal Social Skills' or 'Effective Ways of Applying Hysteria to Problem Solving.' So when I rebelled against the rigid academic program and got caught conducting research on the dean's retarded daughter under the gym steps, my parents once again had to acknowledge my proclivity for serious learning and send me to the public schools where I would receive an education suited to my special talents. Thanks to this decision while a student at Kennedy High I had the privilege of being taught by Fanny Spielberg.

"This former Haight-Ashbury Flower Child, after taking her medication, would thrill me for hours with her stories from literature. Everything I needed to know about the psychedelic, post-Hippie romantics this great teacher taught me! After mastering all the great writers by heart, she saw to it personally that I was accepted by her alma mater, Fabian State. To prep me for the entrance exam, she gave me a practice test, which, to my surprise, turned out to be the same exam that the university gave me. Of course, I did very well. In fact, I was the only student in the university's history to get a perfect score, which I achieved by turning in the test answers, given to me to study. Naturally with brilliant test results like that, I was very well received by the faculty. One of Fanny's faculty friends, Yo Yo Yen, made certain and saw to it that I took all the right courses from all the right professors. Like Fanny, he was very interested in my education, and for six years, until I got my Master's, he saw to it that only the best teachers with the most impeccable credentials taught me!"

The math teacher listened with fascination to everything I said. When I finished, she said simply: "You certainly had an unusual education."

"Yes, I've been most fortunate," I said proudly. "I have been taught by the best, and it seems appropriate that I should in turn teach the best."

"Interesting," she said, staring at me strangely. Once again she made me feel uncomfortable about my blemish, which was obviously disfiguring my otherwise perfect face. After she left, I hid my embarrassment with makeup, then headed for class confident no one else would see my imperfection.

Roger Murphy was amazingly gifted as a teacher. His lectures reflected a depth of understanding that far exceeded anything I could expect. He took some of my key ideas, presented in previous lectures, and he gave new meaning to them.

When I heard him give his now famous "To be or not to be" lecture, I knew immediately a genius was born. At first, I felt uncomfortable seeing a strapping teenager in torn-at-the-knee Levi's and a white shirt and tie stand before my class and deliver a lecture. But the moment I heard him speak in his bass voice those profound words from Shakespeare, my discomfort passed, and I was totally enchanted.

"To be or not to be?" he began. "That my dear class-mates is the question! Is it nobler to suffer the slings and arrows of outrageous fortune or to take refuge against a sea of troubles by fleeing? Those aren't exactly Willie's words, but they certainly are his sentiments. How often he proved this by reaching for a bottle when the slings and arrows got unbearable. But unlike poor Willie, we don't need the bottle. Thanks to modern chemistry, we can sample the pleasures from the supermarket of life. Should we or shouldn't we? To be or not to be?

"As Mame told us in that wonderful musical, let's 'open a new door' and *live!* What Henry Miller said about obscenity in literature—that it isn't there to excite but to point the way to deeper thought—is also true of modern chemistry. So don't allow petty fears (and the Quasimodos in our society) hold you back from enjoying the pleasures of modern science. They are there to point the way to even greater pleasures for those willing to take the leap. To be or not to be? That is the question! But we must answer it wisely, as Auntie Mame did when she opened a new door and left the slings and arrows behind her. In closing, I want to remind you of what Hugo once said, there's nothing greater than 'an idea whose time has come.' That big idea, that powerful thought that's changing the way we look at life, is very simply: To be and not *NOT* to be. For more details and a movie list, please see me after class."

When he finished, the students rose from their chairs and cheered and whistled. The excitement brought tears to my eyes. In all my years of teaching, I have never seen anything like it. Imagine, I, Frank Hamme, was responsible. It was my words and ideas that made this moment possible. How thrilling it is. How special it makes me feel.

I wanted to talk to him after class and tell him how much I enjoyed his lecture, but I couldn't. He was surrounded by students.

After the pats on the back and polite compliments, I overheard them discuss business. During their discussion, Roger agreed to divide the city into sections and sell rights to these sections for 50 percent of the profits. In return for such a cut, he promised to supply the vitamins, the know-how, and, when necessary, the vans. To establish a network quickly, he recommended that another business layer be created. This could be done by dividing each section into smaller parts and selling those parts by school area to other kids for 75 percent of the profits. For quick communication and sales service, they all should have a beeper or cellular phone.

Of course, I was impressed with what I overheard. I never realized how much demand there was for vitamins. But then I was only a public school teacher. What could I possibly know about earning money?

Thanks to my inspiration and Ollie Olson's golden rules Horace Mann was no longer just another middle-class school. Within no time, the student parking lot exhibited all the signs of prosperity. New BMWs, Jags, and Mercedes were quickly replacing the old Fords, Buicks and Dodges.

Although Pepe forbade business transactions in the school, and every teacher was instructed to report any violation, I just ignored it. When beepers went off or when I saw cash transactions in the back of the classroom, I merely looked the other way. For being so considerate, a gracious little gift, usually a thank you card with a little cash, was placed on my desk each week. The first time this happened, I refused to accept the gift. I didn't feel my consideration was sufficient to warrant such kindness. But when the giver insisted, and increased the cash amount, I knew it would be better to accept than to hurt feelings by refusing. Besides, we teachers hardly made enough money to buy an occasional smoke. Why shouldn't we accept a small gift from our more fortunate (and appreciative) students?

Determined to spread Roger's fame (and increase my chances for winning that $10,000 tax-free bonus), I wrote a letter to the President's wife, and told her about his "To be or not to be" lecture. "This exciting moment educationally," I wrote, "which brought tears to my eyes and a standing ovation from the class, would never have been possible if you hadn't had the wisdom and the courage to come up with such an innovative idea." (I almost added that you should eat more chocolate, raspberry cake with whipped cream, but thought that might be a little imprudent.) I went on to say "if other teachers have my success, the educational ramifications should be quite impressive, because it achieves what very few teachers (including myself) can achieve, total class involvement." In closing, I told her how proud I was to be one of the select to teach at this Renaissance school and to participate in this great democratic experiment of bringing real learning to the children of America.

Nine

I was in the newspaper office planning the next issue of *The Inquisitor* when Borlinda entered with a look of angelic serenity. She was hugging her books and was dressed only in white with just a touch of color on her cheeks and lips. When she lowered her books to my desk, her thinly veiled breasts greeted me with a generous hello. She smiled as my head leaped across the desk for a closer view.

"Mr. Hamme, I want you to know I'm the proudest person in the whole world. I have the *biggest*, most *wonderful* secret a person can have." She smiled, her face filling with joy. "I'll bet you'll never guess what it is?"

"Let me try," I said. "Roger has agreed to give his life to God, and the two of you are going off to dark Africa as missionaries for Him."

"Better than that!"

"Better than that?" I said, impressed, wondering what colossal secret this Angel of God had saved for me.

"I'm pregnant," she gushed excitedly. "I, Borlinda Borgia, am going to have a baby!"

I was genuinely surprised. She was the last person whom I'd ever expect to hear that from. This is the girl who was trained to think like a nun. This is the girl who believes the body is the temple of God. Is it possible that she's taken seriously the romantic lessons from literature and has given herself to a man like the great heroines?

"Who's the father?" I asked, fascinated.

"My eternal father, of course."

Sometimes that girl makes no sense. I looked at her puzzled. "Would you be kind enough to explain that, please?"

"Mr. Hamme," she said, padding her stomach proudly. "What I am trying to say is that I've been chosen to bring God's child into the world for the second coming! Imagine me, Borlinda Borgia, selected by God Himself to have an *immaculate* conception."

"*Immaculate conception!*" I said, stunned. "Borlinda," I added like an understanding father, "I think you better have an abortion."

She turned pale, and she backed away from my desk, horrified. "You want me to kill my heavenly child?"

"What about college, and your dream to be a missionary?"

"God obviously has other plans for my life. If He wanted me to go to college, He would've seen to it that one of the Christian colleges that I had applied to would have offered me a scholarship large enough to cover my expenses."

"Maybe He wants you to attend Fabian State."

"Attend a *public* university?" she said, horrified. "No offense, Mr. Hamme, but it's bad enough spending a year here. To spend four years, maybe even longer, in a public university would be *beyond* anything a fine Christian girl like me should ever be expected to endure."

"You should look at it another way. It could be a wonderful place to be an example for God. Have you forgotten already that wonderful poem, 'Pippa Passes'?"

She thought about it for a moment. "You may be right," she said. "But there's still one problem. I *can't* afford it!"

"Get a student loan, like everyone else."

"Mr. Hamme, do you realize how much money it costs to go to college? Do you know how long I'd need to work, as a missionary, to pay that loan back?"

"Who pays them back? Just change your name and get lost in Africa."

"I don't think that's what God expects of me. I think by impregnating me like this He has other plans for my life."

As her teacher and true mentor, it would give me such joy if I could open her eyes to another explanation and turn her into a modern woman by freeing her of her tribal beliefs. "Borlinda," I said, "you must learn to see things with originality. Maybe there is another explanation for your pregnancy. Maybe God wants you to raise money for your education by selling your child."

"Sell the Lord Jesus Christ the Second?" she said, shocked.

"That could've been why He knocked you up."

"I don't think those are *quite* the words I would use to describe my impregnation," she said indignantly.

"Why don't you talk to your minister and ask him about having a church-sponsored auction? If this child turns out to be as perfect as you expect, you should be able to command a *fabulous* price. Maybe even enough to put you through four years of college."

She picked up her books. "I'm sure that's not what God wants," she said, unimpressed. "But I will pray about it tonight, and see where *He* leads me." She then left the office.

It amazed me how impervious those religious types were to new ideas. Getting them into the mainstream of thought is next to impossible. Let's hope through this new complication I can change this and influence that girl to confront life's problems with less piety and more verve.

After school I visited the local adult bookstore to review the latest materials. Some of my best ideas for lectures came while reviewing some of the better publications. I could never understand why the writers, who had such an original and deep understanding of life, weren't more popular. Most of the customers seemed to prefer the pictures and the movies to the printed material. My interests, on the other hand, were literary, and I only went there for the books and the magazine articles. When I did view a movie in the back room, it was only to see a rare classic with a famous cast of actors and actresses—like *The Secrets of Queen Victoria* with those excellent close-ups of the queen's private life.

I was pondering something I had just read on the sex symbols in *Alice in Wonderland*, when I saw Roger approach me.

"Frank!" Roger said. "What a surprise seeing you here!"

"Didn't you know?" I said, pleased to learn that he also appreciated quality entertainment. "This is my favorite bookstore."

"Have you seen the movies yet?"

"No, I usually just come here for the books and magazines."

"Well, there's one flick that'll knock you dead. How about taking a look?"

"Is it suitable for a lecture?"

He was smiling. "Most definitely."

We both squeezed into a room about the size of a phone booth. I never realized before how uncomfortable it was for two. Yet how many times had I seen men, after silently meeting, squeeze into these booths together? Pressed against Roger, it confused me why they would consider such discomfort just to watch a 25-cent movie.

"Wait until you see this one." He dropped a bunch of coins into the machine. The movie was entitled *Slave to Her Men* and it featured none other than *Borlinda Borgia*.

"Why she's better than Vanessa DelRio," I said, impressed.

"She should be. It took three days to film."

"Three days?"

"When you see the big banquet scene, you'll understand why it took so long."

I had to admit I was mesmerized by Borlinda's talent. She performed her duties to the Romans with skill and gave new meaning to the word slave. I particularly liked the close-ups. I don't think anyone has ever filmed such beautiful breasts as hers before. In the big scene, when she exposed them at the banquet, while reading Ovid's *Art of Love,* there wasn't one Roman hand that didn't appreciate them.

"How did Maurice ever do it?"

"My vitamins."

"Amazing!"

"Didn't I tell you you'd like the movie?"

"Such talent."

"I'm sure she has nothing on you."

"Well, I have been told I'm not a bad actor."

"Maybe we should audition together?"

"Do you act too?" I asked, impressed.

"I could," he said, "with the right co-star, and a good smoke."

Roger had difficulty standing without brushing against me. To provide him more room, I opened the door and stepped outside. "Well, let's get together sometime for a reading." I said.

"Sure, Frank. Why not? How about the back seat of my car?"

I knew I would have to top my To-be-or-not-to-be lecture if I wanted to inspire more students like Roger and Borlinda to excel. As a teacher, it was my responsibility to lead my students forward, and, through my untiring dedication, plant within each a seed, which would later grow into something beautiful. One good idea—one well-planted

seed, carefully cultivated—could change a student's life forever, and maybe even *reshape* history. The thought of this
occurring—of me being responsible for such a powerful
idea—was enough to motivate me to search for an exciting
and fresh topic for my next lecture.

But what single idea was large enough and important
enough to achieve such success? Then it came to me in my
sleep. Through a dream, the gods introduced me to a new
Truth. Some of my most profound thoughts came to me in
my sleep, and I learned quickly, if I didn't want to lose them
forever, to jot them down as soon as I awoke.

Some of these thoughts, like the one that inspired today's
lecture on Herman Melville's *Moby Dick*, were too important to forget. If I'm lucky, this one idea, this one dream
could result in an intellectual breakthrough for my students,
which could free them once and for all of their ignorance!
The students obviously sensed my excitement over today's
lecture. A few were nervously chewing gum and blowing
bubbles; others were whispering to each other in anticipation; still others were arranging their heads on their desk in
a listening position. At the precise moment when my eru-
dite thoughts and mellifluous voice filled the room, all conversation ended and all eyes rolled upward as though they
were expecting heaven to open and reveal its glory to them.
After preparing them mentally by briefly exercising their
minds with one of my poems, I launched into my lecture on
Moby Dick.

"*Moby Dick*, class (which you can rent at your favorite
video store) is a very sexy book about a man and his whale.
I had read many comments about the allegorical significance
of the story, but none satisfied me. Then last night, after
watching the movie, I had the most profound revelation,
which came to me in my sleep. I dreamed that Captain Ahab
and Moby Dick were lovers." Suddenly everyone sat straight
up and stared at me in total astonishment. "That's right," I

said. *"Lovers!"* There were a few snickers and smiles, but the majority, overwhelmed by the significance of my thought, merely stared at me with open mouths. "When Ahab was pursuing that magnificent white whale, it was only with one thought in mind," I continued, *"to sadistically violate it!"* I heard gasps of shock, as little minds opened to big ideas. "Never forget. Bestiality *isn't* uncommon in literature, as I pointed out to you before. Good writers in their search for *new* and *interesting* material have often used it as a subject for advancing profound ideas on the human condition. So make no bones about it. Herman Melville was no exception. That man-whale struggle, which he has been thrilling readers with for over a 100 years, is really the exciting struggle of man trying to get it on with a whale."

Borlinda who was gazing in her mirror unexpectedly jumped to her feet, then slapped the boy next to her. She then pulled her chair away from him and sat down again. "Mr. Hamme," she interrupted, after turning her full attention to me. *"Mr. Hamme!"*

I knew by her tone that she wasn't in agreement with my interpretation. At first I tried to ignore her, but I knew by her tone that that wouldn't work today. Her classmates, who usually enjoyed her comments, seemed especially interested in hearing her response. I suspected that they would be furious with me if I totally ignored her. Being the noble teacher that I was, I decided to let her speak and, hopefully through our conversation, lead her to the Light.

"Yes, Borlinda," I said, hiding my annoyance with congeniality. "You have something to add."

"Yes, I do, in fact. My teacher at the Virgin Mary differs with you. According to her, *Moby Dick* is about the eternal struggle of Good and Evil, of the pitiless and cruel Captain Ahab against the strong and free white whale, Moby Dick. When I read the book and saw the movie on television, I never picked up any reference to bestiality."

Oh, the *eternal* ignorance of youth! I try to brighten their lives with knowledge, and they insist on clinging to their ignorance. *Teaching is such a challenge!*

"Borlinda," I began patiently. "You forget something very important. No teacher at an uptight school like the Virgin Mary would ever discuss sex openly. Why just the mention of the word probably sends them running to confession. Therefore, you must free your mind of those things taught to you there, and reread this great book again. You may discover then that I'm right and that *Moby Dick* is a very sexy tale about a man hot after a whale."

At that point a beeper went off. A boy in his haste to leave the room knocked against a girl slouching in her chair. The girl, heavy on medication for a bad cold, slid half-asleep from her chair to the floor, knocking over the boy in front of her, who was leaning back in his chair. Seeing the two entangled on the floor, fumbling clumsily to free themselves, deeply amused the class.

After such an untimely interruption, it would be difficult to recapture the intellectual excitement of my lecture. Rather than try, I wrote a few questions on the board for them to answer, then spent the remaining period making notes on my new revelation about *Moby Dick.*

While basking in the joy of my new revelation, Niko unexpectedly interrupted me. He approached me with the exaggerated look of manliness, insecure males revealed whenever they wanted to bully someone.

"Frank," he said to the point, "I think it's time you pack up and leave."

I merely looked at him and laughed. What else could I do when some Mediterranean aborigine bursts into my classroom and gives me an order!

"You don't understand," he said. "You have no choice. It's either quit or be fired."

"*What* are you talking about?"

"I'm talking about the photos I took of you and Roger in the back seat of his Jag.'"

"So you were the one peering through the window, while we were reading *Alice in Wonderland?*"

"Is that what you were doing?"

"Of course. Surely even a half-wit like you could have figured that out."

"Well, I don't think that's the impression the Board of Education will have after seeing the photos I took."

"You took photos?" I said, confused.

"That's right," he said. "So you have a choice, Frank— you can quit or be fired. You have exactly twenty-four hours to decide which it'll be." He then left triumphantly as though his whole life had been lived for this moment!

Who does that man think he is, coming into my class-room and trying to pressure me to quit? What could he pos-sibly have on film that could make him feel so confident of succeeding. Roger and I were only smoking and reading. The situation was very innocent and proper, unless. . . .

Unless that damn Greek altered the images!

It wouldn't surprise me. It's obvious he would go to any length to get rid of me. In fact, I wouldn't be surprised if he were even using his "romance" with Pepe for that very pur-pose. Well, we'll see who uses whom. I'll show him who has the power around here. I'll get Pepe to castrate him with his sharp Latin teeth.

When I saw Pepe a few minutes later, I didn't need to bring up Niko. Since that Greek entered his life, he seldom talked about anything else. Although I wanted to tell him certain truths about that man, I knew to be direct would be imprudent. Pepe was hopelessly in love. Saying anything too negative about Niko could backfire. So I thought it would be wiser to let Pepe lead the conversation, while I highlighted it with good English sense.

"Sometimes that Greek makes me so angry I can *SCREEEAM!*" Pepe was saying. "Nothing I do pleases him. With Niko, it's always the same. Who do I prefer—Pepe or Pepita? Can't he get it through his thick head that I am both? Why must he try to make me feel guilty for liking both personalities?"

"It's obvious he can't love you very much if he insists on treating you so heartlessly," I said.

But Pepe wasn't listening. He was trapped in his own thoughts. "You know what he told me?" Pepe said, hurt. "You know what that brute said? He said it's not healthy for a 'person' to have two sexual identities. One must go, so the real me could develop. He thinks as long as I remain an impotent man and a nymphomaniac woman I will never fulfill myself. Really the way he talks you would think I was some neurotic, trapped by unnatural needs. The truth is I am a very happy person, who enjoys being a man *and* a woman. Why doesn't he accept this? Why can't that big lug realize that I am HAPPY? *HAPPPPPY!*"

"Obviously it's Niko who has the problem. He is beginning to sound like a classic closet case. Maybe it's time you bring him out."

"That's what I've been *trying* to do! But he always sidesteps me. Do you know what he did after dinner, when I offered him for dessert a choice between Pepe and Pepita? He thanked me, then left. I go to all that trouble to get ready for him, and he merely thanks me, then leaves. That man is heartless! He has no feelings. All he wants is for me to chop off my tits or dick. Oh, I just hate him for the way he treats me. I could just cry!"

"Why don't you slip him something instead?"

"What are you talking about?"

"I mean why don't you ask Roger Murphy for some pills? Maybe he has something that will stimulate his interest."

"Really, Frank. Vitamins? You must be crazy."

"They work on the kids. Why shouldn't they work on Niko?"

"I don't want him alert. I want him to stop resisting. I want him to be *docile.*"

"Well, ask Roger. I'm sure he knows *exactly* the right pill to prescribe. The boy's a regular pharmacist."

"Very well, I'll talk to him. But it's not vitamins that he needs. It's a sledgehammer over the head!"

When I left Pepe's office, Borlinda was removing books from her locker.

"How's the expecting mother?" I said to her.

A look of sublime joy radiated from her. With one question, I succeeded at focusing her entire attention on the most important event in history, her pregnancy!

"Wonderful!" she said.

"Have you discussed it with your pastor yet?"

"Oh yes, indeed. He's very excited about it too. But then why shouldn't he be? This is only the second time in history that there's been an immaculate conception."

"Did he like the idea of an auction?"

"Well, to be honest, Mr. Hamme, no. He felt an auction was inappropriate for his church. The Parish of the Virgin Mary is too orthodox for anything quite so modern. But he did have an idea. He thought we could raffle the child off and split the money fifty-fifty. As an incentive, he would throw in a free baptism for the lucky winner and for me a year's supply of tracts and condoms to distribute at school."

"That may work," I said, impressed. "But is his congregation large enough for a successful raffle?"

"Well, the pastor thought we could always advertise in one of those alternative publications, *The Bobbitt Papers* (if God's second child is a girl) or *The Eunuch Review* (if he's a boy). He thinks many good Christian single men and women would love to have a Child of God for their pleasure."

"Your pastor is right. In fact, if money ever gets tight again, you can always pray for another immaculate conception to finance your studies."

"I'm sure, if it ever becomes a problem, God will show me the way. After all, I am His chosen." She then opened her jacket and revealed her T-shirt which read, "Are You Ready for the Second Coming?" I stared admiringly, at her braless chest which the T-shirt barely hid. "Do you like?"

"Very much!" I said with enthusiasm.

"Good," she said, pleased. "Well, I've got to go. Roger promised me some delicious brownies and $1,000 if I agreed to do another religious epic for Maurice. That's $500 more than the last time. If this continues, I can easily earn enough money making religious epics to pay for my tuition. Oh, Mr. Hamme, aren't I lucky to have such a well-connected business manager like Roger?"

I remembered the Roman banquet scene in the movie, and it brought tears to my eyes to realize that so much talent existed in someone so young. "Oh yes," I said. "You're very lucky to have someone like Roger market your talents."

"I'd like to think it's my Christian character he's marketing."

"You haven't seen the movie then, have you?"

"No, just a few publicity stills," she said. "But I understand the critics liked it very much. In fact, many strangers have approached me and offered me money to perform for them as I had for the Romans. Really, it's only been a few months since I made the movie, and already people are talking about it. If the word continues to spread like this, I could become a star in no time."

"I'm sure you're right," I said. "There's a lot of people out there awaiting your *second* coming."

The President's wife responded to my letter with a phone call. During our brief talk, she told me how delighted she was to receive my letter and how refreshing it was to know that dedicated teachers like me were still in the system. Then, after she hung up, she gave my letter to the press to publish.

Overnight Roger (and I) were famous. Local talk show hosts began to call for interviews. Even the city newspaper sent a reporter to cover Roger (with me, of course) teaching class, and repeating for the benefit of the reporters his now famous "To be or not to be" lecture.

The crowning moment came when Roger was asked to appear on the Kathy Loomba Show and share his thoughts with America. At first he was uncomfortable with this attention and wanted to refuse. But after I told him what a great opportunity it was to use National Public Radio to enlighten the country, he acquiesced. To ease his anxiety, I agreed to join him and help him through the tough spots. For relaxation before our American debut, we shared an herbal cigarette in the car. By the time we had finished, we were both feeling quite cheerful and ready.

Oh, the magic of a healthy smoke!

The hostess, a withering beauty in her fifties, excessively made-up and scantily dressed, ignored me when we entered the studio and gave all her attention to Roger. This surprised me, because I have always been regarded by older woman as quite a catch. But when I observed her with Roger, I knew she was a woman who took her job seriously. Like a true professional, she concentrated on putting him at ease by giving him the type of gracious attention that would help him relax on the air. Of course, when I realized the reason for all the special attention, I sat down by a microphone and did the only thing I could do. I quietly watched. To dazzle the woman with my charm and distract her with my wit would be totally unfair to Roger. This was Roger's big moment and he must shine. By allowing him to shine, I too would shine. After all, I was his creator, the Pygmalion responsible for his magnificent mind.

Although he had a certain raw physical beauty (like most athletic types), it wasn't his beauty that mesmerized people. It was the magic of his words, the wisdom in his ideas. Like me, he had a golden tongue, and like me, he could thrill the world by carefully turning a phrase. What a perfect student he was. What a magnificent teacher and leader he would someday be.

Oh, how proud I was to be his mentor.

Several times during the on-the-air interview, I told the hostess this, but she only listened briefly before turning her full attention to Roger. She was totally under his spell, and he wisely played to it. When her hand reached past the microphone and touched his, he responded with a cute boyish smile that immediately conveyed flattery.

"Tell me, Roger," she said. "Are you wearing a Rolex and a real diamond earring?"

"Yes," he said proudly. "I bought them with the profits from my business."

"You have a business?" she asked, impressed.

"Yes, I sell vitamins."

"Vitamins?" she said. "There's money selling vitamins?"

"Oh definitely. Many of my customers are very loyal. In fact, you might even say they are *hooked* on my pills."

"Then what I heard mustn't be true."

"What's that?"

She leaned very close to him, her breasts pressing against her microphone, as she spoke to America through his microphone. "You don't really plan on teaching after college, do you?"

"Oh, but I do. I want to be a teacher and influence my students just like Mr. Hamme."

"Oh, Roger. What a fine, humanitarian attitude you have."

Her fingers began to play with the hairs on the back of his hand. For a professional hostess, she certainly was nervous. Having two great minds together in one room must overwhelm her. Being the perfect gentleman that he was, Roger did not attempt to pull away. Instead, he wisely used the contact to keep her riveted to what he had to say. While he was repeating some of his ideas, which he had developed in his "To be or not to be" lecture, a man in the adjoining room, separated from us by a glass wall, waved at me frantically, then pointed to the hostess. I immediately assumed that he wanted me to interrupt the conversation with some pithy statement. To accommodate him, I made a few comments about Chaucer and Shakespeare. The hostess merely looked at me, startled, said something about how interesting that all was, then returned to Roger. The man behind the glass stopped waving, and he grimaced while yanking his hair. During a news break, he hurried into the studio, pulled the hostess by her shoulders against her chair, then placed her microphone in front of her.

"America wants to hear you, *NOT* your heartbeat!" he snapped.

At first she was indignant, as I would have been also, if my posture were so rudely corrected in front of guests. But when she realized how unprofessional she had behaved, she began to blush. From that moment on, the interview became formal with her admiring Roger from a distance.

"So tell me, Roger. You believe the big question is 'To be or not to be.' For the benefit of our listeners, would you explain what this big question means?"

"As Mr. Hamme so brilliantly pointed out during one of his lectures on Shakespeare, when Hamlet spoke those words, it was in response to his passionate love for Ophelia."

"His passionate love for Ophelia?" she said, startled. "Mr. Hamme said *that?*"

That was undoubtedly my cue to speak. I cleared my throat with some water. "Yes, that's right. I have learned from my studies of great literature that you must. . . ."

"Thank you, Mr. Hamme," she said. "I remember what you said earlier—*cherchez la femme.*"

"Yes, exactly. I came to that conclusion during my graduate years at Fabian State."

She gave me an angry look, then put her finger to her lips. "Interesting," she said, turning to Roger. "Now Roger, please continue with what you were saying."

"Well, after hearing Mr. Hamme's brilliant lecture on *Hamlet*, I decided to enlarge on his insight. For this I went to the writings of Huxley, Plato, and Miller for my inspiration. But it was really Mame who summed it up so well for me in song with those memorable words—*open a new door!* And that's exactly what I think Shakespeare had in mind when he wrote that soliloquy, open a new door and put the slings and arrows of outrageous fortune behind you. After all, we must remember—To be and not *not* to be is the big idea whose time has come (quoting Victor Hugo)."

"Very well put," she reached across and wrapped her hand around his, and visibly melted upon contact. "Now let's open the wires and hear what our listeners think. First caller, would you like to identify yourself."

"Yes," a young voice said. "My name is Mae Fontaine, and I am in the seventh grade at the Nixon Elementary School in La Jolla. In all my years, I have never heard such a refreshing speaker as Roger. Oh Kathy, do keep it up. I just love it when you have brilliant guests like him."

"Why thank you, Mae."

"Is it all right if I ask him a question?"

"Please do."

"Roger, my 28-year-old boyfriend keeps pressing me to put out for him. He's always telling me you only live once, and life is short and other profound things like that. Well, I want to give in to him, because he's such a hunk, and I am so lucky to have an older man interested in me. But like so many of my girlfriends, I am faced with the big question: To be or not to be his. Well, Roger. I guess what I am asking is this, should I give in to him and open a new door?"

"I can't answer that question for you," Roger said. "That's something you must decide for yourself. But your boyfriend is correct. Life is short, and you do only live once. Therefore, it's foolish to waste your short life worrying about whether you should or shouldn't. You must make a decision based on your feelings, and go with the flow. So the next time your boyfriend corners you, let your response be determined by how you feel!"

"Oh, thank you Roger. I really do appreciate such advice."

"Thank you so much for calling, Mae," the hostess said. "Next caller, would you like to identify yourself?"

"Yes, I am Professor Gerald Hasenfus of Taylor University. In all my fifty years I have never heard so much ignorance paraded so pompously as I have tonight. *Cherchez la femme* in Shakespeare, *nonsense!* Chaucer a transvestite sexist, *incredible!* What we ought to do is open a door (preferably one on an airborne 747) and shove those two idiots out before they corrupt America with their ignorance. Your show, which always has been a big farce, has reached a new low and I congratulate you, Kathy, on your achievement. You have hit rock bottom tonight. Victor Hugo was quite correct. There's nothing more powerful than an idea whose time has come, and that idea whose time has come is simply this: *public education corrupts.* If anyone has any doubts, they should listen to your guests expound on their ignorance."

He then disconnected, as we stared silently at each other, startled by what he had said. I broke the silence with an apt insight about the elitist private school where the caller taught, and dismissed him by defending public education. "What this caller forgets," I began, "is that without the public schools millions of Americans would be illiterate. Many of them would never be able to add and subtract, or even become acquainted with all the great heroes in American history. After all, how many of them have the money to attend an elitist school like Taylor with its questionable selection process and its strange academic requirements? No, America needs the public schools to educate *all* children, not private schools like Taylor to educate just the *chosen* few. What we must realize is that the time has come to free our country of elitist institutions like Taylor where original thinkers like Roger would be banned."

"Thank you, Mr. Hamme. That was very nicely put." She smiled at Roger. "It has been such a pleasure having you on my show, Roger. You must return soon so we can continue this conversation." Again she began to play with the hair on his hand, as the music in the background rose, and she said good-bye to America until tomorrow.

Before leaving the studio, she whispered something to Roger, which made him smile. By the way she looked at me afterwards, I was convinced that she had just said something flattering about me and was embarrassed at possibly being overheard. It was obvious by her aloofness all evening that she was deeply attracted to me, but was too intimidated by my good looks to reveal it directly. I must remember to call her and ask her to lunch. I hate to see women silently suffer.

Overnight Borlinda stripped herself of her makeup and worldly clothes, and became her old holier-than-thou self. The boys, noticing the change, wisely responded to it by avoiding her. It wasn't until Roger entered the classroom that her change really became a concern. The moment she made eye contact with him, her beautiful blue eyes, which had once reflected the soul of an angel, suddenly revealed the crazed look of a fanatic. Instead of behaving in some violent way, she merely walked up to him, handed him a tract, then returned to her seat. Her change concerned me. I wondered what horror could have befallen her to cause such a regression. I immediately wanted to talk to her and see what I could do to salvage what was left of the Borlinda, Erda and I had created.

"Borlinda," I said, after class. "Is something bothering you?"

"Nothing much," she said, nearly in tears, "Roger only ruined my life. That's all!"

"He didn't drop you for someone else, did he?"

"Oh, Mr. Hamme, I wish it were that simple."

"You mean it's worst than that?"

"Oh yes. Much. Remember that Christian movie I told you I made? Well, what I didn't tell you—because I didn't know at the time—was that it really wasn't a Christian movie. My pastor saw it while doing some research for one of his sermons, and he told me all about it."

"Didn't he like your acting?"

"Like it? He was horrified when he learned that that fine Christian movie I thought I had made was just another sex film. Do you realize what this means? It means my life is ruined. *Ruined!* I'll never be able to hold my head up again. All because of Roger. He did it to me. That evil, evil boy deliberately did it to me." The tears were flowing. Instinctively I put my arms around her and comforted her, like a father comforting his daughter during a moment of teenage heartache.

"Your life isn't ruined," I said in my most fatherly voice. "Far from it. The pain will pass and so will the memory. From time to time, life throws us such inconveniences to test our strength, but. . . ."

She pulled away, then looked at me, startled. "Inconveniences?" she shrieked. "I'm pregnant. I am going to have a child out wedlock, after being drugged, degraded and abused for everyone in the entire world to see, and you call it an inconvenience. Really, Mr. Hamme. Sometimes you truly amaze me."

"Believe me, Borlinda. When you're older, you'll realize what a better person you'll be because of this experience. Besides, you can always have an abortion."

"*Abortion?!* You mean *murder* a fetus?! Mr. Hamme, I'm too fine a Christian girl for that."

"Then deliver it and sell it to the highest bidder."

"Who's going to want a child born in such disgrace?"

I was totally exasperated with her, "I don't know what else to suggest."

"That's because I haven't a choice. God made that clear last night. So I guess I'll just have to deliver it and be like Hester Prynne and wear my scarlet letter for the world to see." She then added with a sound of danger in her voice, "*But you can be sure, sure as I'm standing here that I, Borlinda Borgia, will have my revenge!*"

"Have you forgotten what the Bible says about vengeance?"

"You forget, Mr. Hamme. I'm a child of God, and I'm *permitted* this privilege!"

Pepe called me into the office to show me something. "Wait till you see my surprise," he told me before disappearing into his private washroom.

As I sat comfortably in his leather chair, smoking one of his cigars, I wondered what the fag was up to today. When he entered the room again, he was wearing an off-the-shoulder, pure white evening dress, that clung tightly to every girlish curve in his body. A blonde wig, coifed to give roundness to his oval-shaped face, covered his black hair. "Well, what do you think?" he asked. "Do you think I'll be a knock out as Marilyn Monroe at the Horace Mann High Faculty Ball this weekend?"

I had to admit, that if I didn't know better, I would swear he was a woman. His knockers weren't anything like Borlinda's, but they were magnificent! "You're smashing,

Pepe" I said. "I'm sure there isn't a man in the city who wouldn't kill to hump you right now!"

"You think so," he said, pleased. "You really think I look *that* good."

"Definitely."

"Well, I have been known to break a few hearts." He stared at his image in his hand mirror and began to make love to it. His performance made me a little restless for companionship. But being the scholar that I was, it had no lasting affect on me.

After he had thoroughly delighted himself, studying his reflection, he sat next to me.

"Is Niko taking you?" I asked.

"Of course."

"Well, be careful with that man," I said. "I wouldn't want him to break your tender heart again."

"Don't worry, Frank. He's changed. Ever since I started slipping him Roger's vitamins, he's become a different person, so gentle and loving, and. . . ."

"Good," I said, relieved. "He's been anything but that to me."

"I know. I saw the photos."

"He let you see them?" I asked, startled.

"Oh yes. He even let me put them away for safe keeping, after he had seen the photos I had taken of us together."

"You're amazing."

"Now tell me, Frank," he said. "How's that fascinating article on Chaucer coming along?"

"Well, thanks to you, Pepe, I have a whole new insight into one of the characters," I paused to collect my thoughts. "I think," I began, "the Prioress was Chaucer in drag."

"Chaucer?" he said. "In drag? *How original!*"

"As straights like me know," I continued, "no real woman could ever be as feminine as she. That's because only a man knows what an ideal woman ought to be. Now take you, for example. As convincing as you are in that gown, you still don't come off as a woman. Why? Because you're *perfect!* No woman could ever be as feminine and exciting as you are right now. Not because women aren't feminine and exciting, but because you being a man know what a real woman ought to be, and when you become a woman, you bring with it all the feminine charms men expect in women. That's why you're so successful. Men recognize your perfection, and appreciate it. Yet *real* men know you're an impostor. Because real women *aren't* perfect!"

"You know, Frank. That makes a lot of sense. That article is going to be one hell of a great piece when you are finished."

"I agree, Pepe. I think it's going to change the way we read the classics."

Ten

Roger's popularity grew after the public radio broadcast. Overnight he began to receive letters from across the country. Like a wise businessman, he wanted to use this opportunity to market his products nationally. But after lengthy meetings with his Jamaican suppliers, he was encouraged to restrict his business to just the local schools, because of complicated franchise agreements. This proved to be good advice. Within a month, he made so much money from expanding into all the public schools that he was able to buy a Rolls Royce! When I realized how much money he made selling pills, I begged him to hire me, but he politely refused.

"You belong in the classroom," he said wisely. "You mustn't corrupt yourself yielding to materialism. Vitamin pill salesmen are a dime a dozen, but someone with your mind and your understanding is rare. No, I need you (*I mean*, the world needs you) as a teacher preparing kids to become professionals like me!"

He, of course, was right. My calling was to teach, not to sell pills. I accepted his black Jaguar that he gave me as a gift in appreciation for all I had done for him, because I wanted to have something of his to remind me always of the very special person I had created.

About the same time Roger began to enjoy his success, a curious thing began to happen. Students were beginning to faint in class. At first, there was only an occasional student once or twice a week, but by the second month, there were four or five a day. But it wasn't just in our school. All the public schools were having the same problem. Many teachers were confused as to the cause. Some blamed it on the ventilation, others on the students' diet, and still others on home problems. Since there were so many opinions and so few facts, during a faculty meeting, I suggested that we should buy camcorders and tape the faintings. Maybe then we could obtain some clues to the cause. Pepe thought the idea had merit and decided to discuss it with Phyllis. Phyllis who liked the idea sent memos to all the school principals, requesting them to buy camcorders with the money reserved for supplies. Several members of the community upon hearing about the plan published inflammatory letters to the editor, but Phyllis (and the school board), unmoved by such public pressure, did the sensible thing.

They just ignored their critics!

Since Pepe had only enough money in his budget to buy one camcorder, only one person would be able to tape. The person chosen, in Pepe's opinion, must have a grasp of psychology and a flexible nonteaching schedule that allowed him/her the freedom to respond quickly to emergencies. The only person at Horace Mann with those special qualifications, after carefully evaluating each faculty member, turned out to be the counselor. Pepe's real reason for selecting Niko—which he confessed to me privately—was to have an excuse to work closely with him during this crisis.

When Niko was told that he would be the cameraman, he protested, and said a few unkind things about my idiotic ideas. But Pepe, who recognized my sensibilities, slipped Niko a vitamin in his Coke and quickly brought Niko to his senses. Thanks to all the Cokes Niko drank, it didn't take long before he was responding to all the emergencies with enthusiasm.

I had to admit Pepe made a good decision. From the beginning, Niko revealed a professionalism that impressed even me. Like an artist, Niko filmed his subjects from unusual angles—standing on chairs, window sills, or lying on the floor—in search of that elusive perfect shot. Afterwards, he moved the students by stretcher to the gym and placed them on mats. As they awoke, he again filmed them. By the end of the second week, Niko had over a dozen tapes of twisted bodies in interesting and sometimes even provocative positions without one solid clue to the cause of the faintings. The only persistent pattern recorded was the way some students fell and exposed themselves. This immediately suggested Freudian overtones and convinced me (and Pepe) that Niko might be onto something important.

It was Phyllis' idea, after talking to Pepe, to do a general study on the faintings with all the schools sharing their findings. Through such a joint effort, it was hoped a pattern might be observed that would identify the cause of the problem. I became very excited about the study upon learning about it. By providing the schools with a new method for conducting scientific study, I was making an important contribution to medical research. I could see it now in the *New England Journal of Medicine*—"Frank Hamme, Horace Mann High lit teacher, discovers a new approach to the study of fainting, *The Hamme Camcorder Method.*" Recognizing the brilliance of this contribution made my head reel. Only a few American teachers could match what I have just done to advance general knowledge. I really must contain my genius. My greatness could intimidate my colleagues and absolutely *destroy* morale at school.

Despite all Niko's excellent film footage, I still couldn't help thinking that we might be on the wrong track. There could be a very simple explanation for the faintings, which eluded us because of its obviousness. This thought haunted me, while listening to Pepe complain.

"Poor Niko," Pepe said. "All that filming, and no real clues. I wish I had some answers. Our gym is beginning to look like a military hospital with students lying everywhere."

"You know, Pepe. Maybe the reason we haven't found an answer is because we are looking in the wrong direction."

"Wrong direction?"

"Exactly," I said. "I'm beginning to believe—based on my gut feelings—that the students might be faking it."

"Why would they want to do that?" he said, startled.

"Simple," I said, proud of my thought. "To escape *dull* classes! Of course, I realize some students (particularly mine), because of the enormous mental pressure I subject them to, are genuinely exhausted. The majority, though, are faking it. Maybe the faculty would benefit from learning some of my techniques for making their lessons more interesting. It *could* make a difference."

"You forget, Frank," he said. "Not everyone is as well-endowed as you." He glanced at the clock on the wall. "Now you'll have to excuse me. I have an important meeting with Niko, and I must get back to the office."

For nearly two weeks, it was the same. Every time I had my students entranced by my hypnotic brilliance, a voice on the intercom would awaken them. "Mr. Papalodopoulos, you are wanted in the gym." "Mr. Papalodopoulos, please contact the principal." "Mr. Papalodopoulos, there's an emergency in Room 201." It got to the point that just the mention of his name was enough to make me want to rip the intercom from the wall. If other teachers took more interest in their subjects and gave the same attention to their students as I, we wouldn't have all these kids faking faintings all day.

I removed the metronome, and set it on my desk. "Please class," I implored. "Concentrate." I then started the metronome. "That's it. Sway with the pendulum. Left, right, right, left. Excellent." When all the heads were moving in time to the metronome, I returned to my lecture.

"It's a well-known fact," I began. "Dostoyevsky, to write so exactly and dramatize new ideas so originally had to use hallucinogenics for inspiration. No one could ever have perceived life like that without the use of mind-benders. Yet as entertaining as he is, as provocative and powerful as his thoughts might seem to sophomoric intellectuals, he is still first and foremost a *psychedelic* writer. In contrast, two especially gifted Post-Hippie Romantics worth noting, whose works reflect a true vision of life, are serial killer Norman Menchetti who wrote that brilliant novel, *A Housewife's Fantasy*, and ex-geisha Satoru Ohtsuki who wrote that sensitive love story, *Tales from a Cambodian Brothel*."

A siren was suddenly heard screaming in the streets. At the same time, inside the school, a voice on the intercom cried: "Mr. Noriega, you're wanted in the gym. It's an emergency. Repeating: An *emergency* in the gym!."

The students sprung to life, as though awakened by the harsh ringing of an alarm clock, and they were on their feet and at the window before I could stop them.

"Look, those men in white are carrying out bodies."

Several boys opened the windows, sending a blast of polar air into the classroom, dropping the temperature from ninety to fifty degrees in a matter of moments.

"Holy shit," another student said. "There are five ambulances out there. *And two more are coming down the street!*"

"Let's check it out!"

I must get the class' attention again. They must learn to ignore such distractions. "Damn it, class," I shouted, picking up the metronome to throw at the first student who disobeyed me. "Get away from that window!"

Wisely they did—by leaving the room. I really must learn to be more specific when I give orders. I didn't want them to *leave!*

I closed the windows, and watched the men load bodies into the ambulance. Despite my anger, I had to admire those kids for having the courage to fake it. Only genuine students, dedicated to learning, would go that far to make a point.

Still, these interruptions are a scandal. How will I ever rise to the top of my profession, be acknowledged by the world as the brilliant man I am, if I must constantly fight unreasonable interruptions to the beautiful rhythm of my lectures? Pepe must stop pandering the teachers and start demanding from them complete professionalism. If I were principal, things would be different. Those kids would have no reason to faint. They would be doing what they ought to be doing right now—*learning!*

"Mr. Hamme, Mr. Hamme," Borlinda said, hurrying into the room. "Have you heard? Mimi Flicop died. She just passed out in Mr. Rosenblatt's class, and never came to again."

"I would too if I had to listen to that teacher all day," I said. "Did you know that he blames Hitler for World War II? What that teacher forgets (as several German scholars have recently documented) is that World War II could've been avoided if the Jews had been just a little more compliant. In fact, we wouldn't be having so many problems in the Middle East today, if Hitler had his way. I really think someone should talk to that man."

"You can be certain, Mr. Hamme, that Mr. Rosenblatt isn't to blame for what happened to Mimi," she said confidently

"Well, if he isn't, how do you explain that I rarely have such problems in my class? No, Borlinda. You're wrong. Thanks to the quality of my lectures and those wonderful vitamins the students take, my students are always alert and interested. Other teachers have such problems, because they are *boring* kids."

"Mr. Hamme," she said impatiently, "when are you going to realize that your peculiar Truth isn't what's going to make the difference. It's *my* Truth—revealed to me through the Word of God—that will change history. Mimi's tragedy is that she died before accepting the Lord Jesus Christ as her savior, before I could baptize her in the Word. And now it's too late for her. Now like some overbaked suckling pig, she's roasting in hell, *screaming* for mercy. Well, it serves her right. She should've listened to me when I spoke—she and all her silly friends should've gotten on their knees and repented when I warned them. But no, they *preferred* the fast life. Well, they'll just have to suffer for it. All of them—for eternity!"

I was startled by her tone, which was filled with malice as sharp as a razor. "Borlinda," I said, concerned, "you really must get rid of that Christian fervor, and become pragmatic like the rest of us and go with the flow. If you continue like this, you'll be raving maniac."

"I suppose it would please you," she said sarcastically, "if I were to become like Mimi Flicop?"

"Well, thanks to my influence, her life wasn't totally in vain. After all, she did create some brilliant Dada art. In fact, I wouldn't be surprised if her uncommissioned paintings were someday placed brick by brick next to the Vermeers and da Vincis in the Washington National Gallery of Art."

"Better still," she said, "next to the Kandinskys and De Koonings with the inscription: 'She owed it all to Roger Murphy's vitamins.'"

I was alone in the newspaper office editing my 30-page essay on Transvestite Sexism in the *Canterbury Tales*, when Roger entered. Watching this healthy-looking boy approach me like an athlete overdosed on vitamins and exercise made me wonder why he never showed any interest in girls. Certainly a boy as attractive as he should have many girl friends. Is it possible that he is like me (a born leader) who fulfills himself guiding others to the Light?

Roger smiled, as though he knew what I was thinking, then offered me my favorite hand-rolled cigarette. After one drag, I was ready for a lift off.

"You're quite a man," he said unexpectedly. "I bet you really know how to please women."

I thought of the many professional women who had the good fortune of knowing me. "You're right," I said proudly. "I've made many women very happy for the few minutes we were together."

"Is that all you gave them—just a few minutes of your time?"

"A few minutes was usually all I could afford. After all, I'm only a poorly paid teacher."

"I bet there are many men and women who'd be willing to pay *you*."

"You're probably right," I said. "But I'm very selective."

"You should be. You have too much to offer to throw it away on just anyone."

"You know for a person so young, you are extremely wise," I said after greedily inhaling my cigarette.

"I learned it all from you, Mr. Hamme. Everything I am I owe to teachers like you."

Oh, what a *wonderful* young man he is! To think this extraordinary student-teacher, this brilliant businessman, is *mine* to mold. *How lucky I am to have him!*

I inhaled the cigarette again. This time I blasted off like a rocket, leaving my body lifelessly behind to slip to the floor.

When I awoke, it was evening, and I was lying on my stomach with my pants pulled down to my ankles. Embarrassed, I quickly got to my feet, pulled up my pants, and stealthily left the school, hopeful no one had discovered me in my disgraceful state. In all my years, I have never pulled my pants down in my sleep. What could've possibly gotten into me?

Pepe had changed since the Horace Mann Faculty Ball. All he talked about was Niko—that gentle, masculine man with the soul of a poet, the body of an athlete, and the intelligence of a god. Since he had known Niko, all other men (and there were *many*) ceased to exist. If Pepe weren't such a special friend, if I didn't have a genuine regard for him, I would have lost all patience with him. Here I was the most beautiful specimen of manhood around, and that sexual joke ignores me for that Greek peasant. Although I would strongly object if Pepe ever touched me, what I couldn't understood is why he never tried. My only explanation is that he felt I was too unattainable and that he would only hurt himself reaching for something he could never have. Maybe that might explain his peculiar attraction to a man of lesser talent (and beauty) like Niko.

"You know, Pepe," I said, satisfied with my explanation, "you and Niko were the talk of the ball. After Saturday night, Niko won't ever be able to return to the closet again."

"You can thank Roger's pills for that," Pepe said. "That wonderful boy had just the right one for the occasion, and when Niko was at the men's room, I just slipped it into his drink. The rest you and everyone else saw on the dance floor."

"Phyllis is going to be green with envy when she hears about you two."

"That's very unlikely. She's so caught up in her own life that she hasn't time for me anymore."

"Is she still walking the straight and narrow with Borlinda's mother?"

"Oh yes, they do everything together. I think Phyl has finally found Ms. Right."

"Doesn't that bother you just a little?"

"Don't be silly. Why should it?"

"Don't you miss all the good times you two used to have together?"

"It's true. Phyl and I had some great times together, but you must remember. As attractive as Phyl is in her military attire, and as sexy as she is in her mean moods, she is still a woman! As a woman, she can never please me in that special way a man like Niko can. So my answer to your question is, no I don't miss her. *I have Niko now!*"

As delighted as I was with Pepe's success at changing Niko (and Phyl's skill at amusing Mrs. Borgia), I knew once the effects of the health pills wore off, Niko could easily change into an angry Borlinda. I had to be certain—for the sake of their romance—that Pepe understood the urgency of continuing Niko's vitamin treatment.

"So tell me, Pepe, what's Niko like when the vitamins wear off? Is he still as romantic?"

He looked at me, annoyed for pointing out a reality he preferred to ignore. "Well, not exactly. But Roger and I are working on that." He then changed the subject, and asked my opinion on how to improve things at school.

I took advantage of this moment to expound on one of my brilliant thoughts on public education. "You know, Pepe, I've been thinking, If we lengthened the school day until 9:00 P.M., we could probably solve many of the problems we face. Six hours a day isn't nearly enough time for us to cover everything we need to. You may want to present this idea to Phyllis. Of course, I think teachers should be remunerated sufficiently for the extra time."

"That isn't what I was referring to. What I was referring to were the faintings, more specifically, Mimi's death."

"You can't imagine how saddened I was to learn about her untimely death. What a loss she's going to be to the art world. How many talented students like her will we have to lose before the public catches on. I agree with the health department doctors. If our school had a clinic with a full-time medical staff, we could've prevented this tragedy. But parents seem to object. They think the schools should only focus on education. Well, you and I both know, that's nonsense. The public schools must reach out in all directions, and be all things to the entire community. In fact, I think I will write the President's wife about this, and even ask the IRS to step up its collection procedures in order to make more funds available for the schools. Spending $640 billion annually on education is not enough. We need more if we are to have bigger and better schools and end all these faintings."

"I personally don't think it's that simple, and I'm sure the Board of Education doesn't either. In fact, if these faintings don't end soon, they could lead to a major embarrassment for the public schools."

"You worry too much, Pepe. That'll never happen. What you need to do is to forget your work and have a long weekend romp with Niko somewhere. I know it seems strange that a workaholic like me should be saying this. But the difference between you and me is that I don't worry about my work like you. I examine my problems objectively with a certain emotional detachment. But you, Pepe, you worry about them, and that isn't healthy."

"That's because I have good reason to worry. Those faintings are a serious problem. Even Phyllis agrees, and she is putting enormous pressure on us principals to find the cause. But none of us know where to look. Some blame the drinking water. Others the ventilation. And still others the lunch food. One thing is for sure. There's no pattern to it. At Roosevelt High the entire senior class was rushed to emergency after a lunch break, which makes a strong case against the food. On the other hand, at Wilson Elementary, seven students were hospitalized after morning recess. The only symptom they all have in common is that the kids faint and when they awake, they have no memory of what happened. Of course, there is Mimi who never did awake."

"Please forgive me for being redundant, Pepe. But as I told you before I think the problem is primarily academic. I seldom have kids fainting in my class. But that's because my lessons are interesting and provide the type of information students find relevant. If other teachers did the same, Horace Mann would never have all these faintings, and it could become a true Renaissance school in the classic sense. Maybe I should do a little research for you (maybe even a newspaper piece). It might help in your search for answers."

"That's very kind, Frank. But I think there's more to the problem than academic neglect."

"Well, I still would like to do an article for you now that I've finished my piece on Chaucer."

"*You finished Chaucer?*"

"Yes, and I'm very pleased with the results and most eager to submit it for publication. Yet, despite the scholarly importance of my research, I'm willing to put the article aside temporarily and assist you with your problem. We've been friends too long. Not helping you in your time of need would be heartless."

"How thoughtful, Frank. I just don't deserve such loyal friendship."

Without knocking, Niko burst into the room. As soon as he entered, Pepe changed. His voice had melody. He danced toward the man. If I wouldn't have been there with my masculine presence, he would've probably leaped into Niko's arms. Niko instinctively stepped back. "Please, Pepe," he said. "We must talk. Another student is ill, and we've got to talk seriously."

Pepe's glow vanished. I wasn't sure if it were because of Niko's rejection or the student's illness. "Is it serious?" Pepe asked, concerned.

"His parents think it's the same thing that killed Mimi," Niko said. "Of course, they're very worried."

"What did you tell them? How did you calm them?"

"I did the only thing I could. I told them that we were investigating the matter, and just as soon as we have enough film footage, we will get in touch with them."

"Oh Niko, I hope this doesn't turn out to be some horrible tragedy—some embarrassing scandal that will destroy the public schools."

"No chance, Pepe," Niko said. "There's too much money in public education. You can be sure there'll be a cover up before that ever happens."

Pepe smiled, and there was love in his eyes again. His entire attention was focused on Niko. "That was very comforting, Niko. Thank you."

"I was telling Pepe, before you entered, that I think the kids are faking it, and that the problem is obviously academic."

"Thank you, Frank," Pepe said. "Don't you have an article to write?"

I was quick to catch the hint. It was obvious the Latin bombshell wanted to be alone with her King Kong, and she found my presence constraining. So I departed like a gentleman and left the two lovers alone to maul each other.

It took nearly four months, but in those four months I had succeeded at turning my staff into trained journalists with an eye for the news. Seeing them collect information—from desk drawers, purses, pockets, and car trunks—really thrilled me. With all the finesse of professionals, they brazenly tape-recorded private conversations and photographed interesting liaisons. In gathering information, they followed my instructions explicitly and hid in closets, doorways, under desks and tables—listening, writing, photographing, and taping everything fit to print.

As a reward for all their hard work, they delighted their classmates with excellent articles like "A Teacher's Secret," "The Virtues of Revenge," and "Reducing PMS Discomforts through Clitoral Stimulation." Although some of the teachers objected to these articles and felt they were inappropriate for a school newspaper, I, of course, disagreed. "Our newspaper must open its door to *all* views," I wrote in my editorial, "and keep nothing out, except censorship!"

When I told my staff my plans for our next issue, I knew by their eagerness they were ready for the big time.

"This is going to be a major article," I told them. "So get me all the facts you can to support my point. I want every reader to know that the cause for the faintings at Horace Mann is *boring* teaching!"

"Do you want pictures?"

"Everything," I said.

For two weeks, I locked myself in my apartment, and worked until early morning, transcribing tapes. Occasionally a tape of one of my lectures was included among the tapes, undoubtedly to remind me to provide some solid examples of good teaching. Since I thought it was a good idea, I included my lecture on Agatha Christie to make my point about the importance of careful research. "To the world," I wrote, "she was known as a respectable English mystery writer, but to friends and family she was a former Sicilian gun moll who retold with an English twist tales from her early years in Palermo."

I even included photos of me teaching. Unlike the photos from other classes, those taken in my room didn't have all that hand-waving and smiling. Instead, they were dignified pictures of a brilliant-looking teacher who was mesmerizing his students with his profound insights.

I was so impressed with the material gathered that I asked my staff to expand their research to include other schools as well. Once the word was out about my project all types of documented material poured in. Armed with facts, I put together without mercy an analysis of the problem. I gave names, examples, dates, and linked the faintings to specific lectures. When I wasn't sure of my facts, I made them up and resorted to a journalistic trick of attributing my statements to an unnamed source, whom I pledged never to identify for the privilege of his statement! It was a brilliant indictment of modern teaching, which placed the blame for the high dropout rate, the faintings, the crime, and all the other social problems in America exactly where it belonged: on those teachers who failed to make their lessons *entertaining* and *original!*

The response to my article in *The Inquisitor* was immediate. Upon publication, every teacher in the school was talking about the article. When I reached the faculty lounge, I could hear them excitedly share opinions.

"How dare that idiot make such a statement about me. I'm going to sue. I'm going to call my attorney, and *SUE!*"

"You don't have a case, Mary Lou, he has tapes."

"But he took everything out of context."

"You forget. You committed a Hamme error by asking your class to think. That isn't allowed in a Renaissance school. What you must do is make profound observations like Dostoyevsky is a psychedelic writer or *Moby Dick* is a story about getting it on with a whale. You do that and you'll have your students sitting on the edge of their seats waiting for the next episode, instead of fainting."

"She's right, Mary Lou. You must learn to be original like Hamme and open *new* doors to *new* ideas. Otherwise, you will be doomed for the rest of your life to repeat the stale truths of the scholars before you. So open a new door, and. . . ."

That's when I decided to enter and accept their congratulations in person.

When I entered, all conversation stopped. I paused by the door, as every eye settled on me and waited for the applause. But there was none. There was only a heavy silence, which abruptly ended with all the teachers rising and leaving at once, almost in a rush.

How flattering! My presences so overwhelms them they can't even speak anymore. All they can do is run from the room like the insignificant creatures they are to avoid the possibility of embarrassing themselves trying to have an intelligent conversation with me.

I sat in the chair, picked up *The Inquisitor,* and reread my article for the sixth time today, before reporting to my class.

When I entered the classroom, I discovered that even my students were talking about the article.

"My mom read your article," one student said to me. "And she plans to come to school and talk to my teachers about some of those things you said. She agrees with you. She thinks it's shameful that teachers should bore us. She too would fake a fainting to get out of some of those classes you described."

"I must meet your mother sometime," I said. "She sounds like a very wise woman."

"Well, my daddy thinks you're crazy! He says math and science are important, and should be taught like they are."

"Obviously your father doesn't recognize the significance of my research," I said in defense. "If he did, he would want to discuss it with me seriously."

"Hey, Mr. Hamme," a boy said. "Mr. Rosenblatt thinks you're crazy too. He says many of the teachers you call bor-ing—because they expect us to learn axioms based on 'tired-out, old research'—aren't boring but instead, interesting and capable."

"Young man," I said, trying to conceal my impatience with such a shallow view of education. "You are. It is true, only a student. For that reason, I can't expect you to fully understand. But what I said *is* correct. Perhaps someday you'll agree and you'll realize that a good teacher (as I so clearly am) *always* encourages original thought by refusing to clutter minds with tired-out, old research. It's only by maintaining an uncluttered mind that you are able to discover True Reality. That's why I never force you to master anything. Instead, I try to show you different ways of seeing life so that you can discover your own Truth. Good teachers who do this never have serious problems in their classes because their students aren't trying to escape the tedium of academic restraint by *faking* a fainting! Instead, their students are absorbing, growing, and *flying* through the universe like astronauts, penetrating the unknown."

"Oh, man," one student said, applauding. "That's *heavy!*" Others joined in. I could feel their full approval, as they stood and whistled and made loud, wonderful sounds. I made a gentle bow, and felt for the first time the joy of being appreciated for what I was.

Because of the strong emotional response from some, I knew I had written a truly brilliant article, and for that reason I decided to submit it to the city newspaper where it was immediately published. Within a few hours after publication, I began to hear from everyone (reporters, parents, and even the local university). The world finally stopped revolving around others long enough to notice me. I always knew one day it would happen, and I would really become famous. Now that the day has finally come, I must start making notes for my biographers.

Oh, how demanding success is!

An unexpected faculty meeting was called on the same day the article appeared in the city newspaper. I was very excited about the meeting, because I was certain it would give me the opportunity to discuss some of my ideas with the staff. When I reached the faculty room, I paused outside to listen to the conversation. To my surprise, the teachers weren't talking about me. Disappointed, I immediately entered and, as I did, they stopped talking and stared at me silently. Even Pepe—who was punctual for the first time this term—also just stared.

When I sat down in a vacant front-row chair, the teachers did a very kind thing, they all rose and moved to the back of the room. They obviously wanted to make certain I had enough space to stretch out in. I took advantage of some of this extra space and spread my legs, thrilling Pepe with my manliness (which, compared to his, seemed small, but because of my superb, all-male packaging was quite noteworthy).

Oh, how lucky I am to be so special!

"I have called this meeting," Pepe said, coming directly to the point, "because of the rising concern over what is happening in our schools. Most of us are very upset about the faintings, particularly the death of Mimi, and for good reason. She was well loved by all. True, she was a little wild, and true, she wasn't our best student. But little did we know, until we got the medical report, that a dreadful virus was destroying her. Some worry that the virus is spreading, but thanks to Frank," and he politely smiled at me in that special way only a true friend might, "thanks to Frank, we have a new explanation for the faintings. What's happening here, and in other schools, as he so carefully documented, isn't the result of a virus, but academic neglect."

At that point almost every teacher in the room started talking at once. They were obviously so impressed with my contribution to a major problem that they all wanted to be the first to compliment me.

"Please," Pepe said. "One at a time. We've got to have order."

"Look, Pepe. I am becoming quite impatient with that moronic lit teacher. I don't like it one bit having my classroom remarks distorted. I had prepared a very thoughtful lecture on Madame Curie's dedication to science, and that lunatic (and I am referring specifically to *Hammy*) totally twists it out of shape in that outrageous article of his. True, Madame Curie's life isn't as colorful as Frank's. But that still doesn't give him grounds to condemn me (and I quote from Frank's article), 'that by forcing students to admire the life of a madcap scientist like Curie, who deliberately exposed the environment to radioactive elements, teachers like her aren't lifting children to new intellectual heights, but instead dropping them into an environmental wasteland.'" The teacher paused. *"Have you ever heard such nonsense?* Only a madman out to discredit Great Western Achievement would make an outrageous statement like that."

"I too resent the way he distorted what I said," another teacher began. "When I quoted Thomas Jefferson as saying, 'When in the course of human events, it becomes necessary for one people to dissolve the political bonds which have connected them,' I wasn't claiming that Jefferson wanted to plant in the Constitution an anarchic thought, which could be used later to overthrow America. Only an idiot would think that. But I guess that's what we're dealing with, *an idiot!* Maybe that's why everything Frank says is so contrary to common sense, so terribly wrong or illogical. It makes me wonder what happened to his brain when it was being created!"

Their reaction horrified me. It reminded me of what Seneca had said about the rough road that leads to the heights of greatness. There was no question that I was on that road, with my inferiors clawing at me jealously. Wasn't this the fate of the great, the Kants and Khomeinis? Weren't they also dismissed by some, because they dared to be different and seek new, instead of well-accepted ideas?

"Do you have anything to say, Frank?"

"There's nothing to say. I think I said it all so well in my article. I leave it to the world to judge, not a few *insignificant* teachers."

"Listen to who calls *us* insignificant! One needs a *microscope* to see your brain!"

I rose. "There's no point in listening to this. It's obvious that all of you are too emotional to view my contribution objectively. Therefore, we'll just have to finish this discussion at another time, when you are a little more clearheaded and open-minded about what I might write."

"You bet we'll finish it—*in court!*"

"Do you really think you can control me with threats of legal action?" I said, annoyed.

"We'll do more than that if you don't shut up."

"No one shuts up a Hamme, because I have Truth and family tradition on my side. As an English gentleman with ancient roots, my responsibility is to speak out—to *enlighten* the world. If in the process a few of you are exposed as charlatans, then let it be. History will prove me right, *because I am a Suscrofa!*"

"Don't you mean wild boar like Sus scrofa?"

I ignored the remark and left with my aristocratic elegance, while they shouted among themselves like the plebeians they were.

Eleven

The following day the teachers were openly hostile to me. All I needed to do was to look at them, and four-letter words would explode from their mouths. I never realized until then how ugly small people could be. It made me feel sorry for them—for their dull and useless existence.

If only they would open the door to friendship, I could change all that by enriching their lives with my superior knowledge. Was that so difficult for them to do? Or was that difficult to do, because it would require them to acknowledge their inferiority?

Well, whatever the reason. It's *their* problem. What makes me special is that I continue despite the resistance, and still achieve. If they chose to dislike me for having the courage to tell the truth, then let them. I will be strong and ignore them, and go on without them. I have my work, and that's more important than their friendship.

So instead of spending my free time in the faculty room sharing ideas with the staff as before, I spent it in the newspaper office reviewing the next issue of *The Inquisitor*.

Squeezed between two fascinating articles—"The Ultimate Suppository for Hemorrhoids" and "The Proper Dress for a 'Ball'"—was a short article entitled "The

Colombians' Revenge," which someone tried to sneak past my eagle eye. The article read like a warning to the Jamaicans and those dealing with them.

"The faintings at school weren't faked as one idiot thinks, but instead caused by drug contamination—the Colombians' revenge for the Jamaicans' move into our territory."

After reading the article, I was very confused. First, I never remembered hearing anything about the Jamaicans wanting to leave their beautiful island for Colombia. But more important, how was such a move relevant to what was happening at Horace Mann? Where do these kids get those ideas? I wish they would stop writing such absurd stories. I guess I'll just have to remind them again about the importance of accuracy. They must understand to be taken seriously as journalists, they have got to be accurate, accurate, accurate! I killed the article immediately and replaced it with a short piece on graffiti, or, as I preferred to call it, "Aphorisms on the Bathroom Wall."

When I left school for the day, a fair-haired man in sunglasses and a dark suit called me to his car.

"Hey, you," he said. "Come here."

I leisurely turned toward the man in the inexpensive-looking, white car, and in my aristocratic English voice asked: "Are you talking to me, sir?"

"That's right," he said, pointing to the school. "You work there?"

I was disappointed that he didn't recognize me from my newspaper photo. "I do," I said proudly. "I'm Frank Hamme, the English teacher. You may have heard of me. My article on. . . ."

"Of course," he interrupted. "You're Roger Murphy's teacher."

"That's right," I said, disappointed that he didn't immediately recognize me. "And I'm also the writer who. . . . "

"I understand Roger has a very successful business," he said, interrupting again.

"He does," I said. "His vitamins are in great demand. It's amazing how successful he's become selling a few pills."

"Amazing," he replied.

"As you have probably heard, my skills as a teacher. . . ."

"You don't by any chance know who supplies him, do you?" the man *again* interrupted.

"No," I said. "In fact, I've never seen his entire product line. But I do know his supplier has Jamaican connections, and does provide him with everything he needs to manufacture his vitamins locally. One of these days I'm going to try his pills. They do the most wondrous things for the kids. After taking them, they become so alert and bright. I really do agree with the superintendent. If the schools saw to it that all the children were given nutritious meals and a daily supply of vitamins, it could make a tremendous difference in their grade average. Yes, I must remember to write the school board about this."

"That's very sensible," he said. "Now back to Roger. Do you know where these eh. . .vitamins are manufactured?"

"To be honest," I said. "I've been so busy with my duties as a teacher that I can't say I've ever asked him. Preparing my lectures requires all my concentration. It's so important that a teacher of my status gives his full attention to researching his lectures. So although I am very much interested in the activities of my students. . . ."

"Incidentally," he *again* interrupted, "do you know a Borlinda Borgia?"

"She's also one of my students."

"Well, thanks for your time."

Before I could inquire into his purpose, he drove off.

I had stopped smoking in school between classes when the students began to tease me about the strange smell in my classroom. Although I knew it really didn't matter to them, I still wanted to set a good example and not be like them, and smoke in the building during school hours. Since it was a cold and overcast morning, I decided to sit in my Jaguar where, protected from the weather, I could bury myself in the soft leather seat, surrounded by the romantic music of Schoenberg, and enjoy an herbal smoke.

While smoking, I began to admire all the foreign cars in the student parking lot. It amazed me that Roger's success could bring so much prosperity to so many students. I was pleased to realize the American Dream was still a possibility. Sometimes when I looked at my paycheck after taxes, I was certain that starvation was all the government had for me, that my condo and Jag would be my only rewards for my great sacrifices to humanity. During such moments, I would become depressed and wish I were hustling vitamins like my students so that I could have extra money for some of life's pleasures. But when I seriously thought about it, I knew Roger was right. Someone with my talent belonged in the classroom.

What other profession allowed me the opportunity to turn a Mimi Flicop into a painter, a Roger Murphy into a teacher, and an Igor Ivanovich into an actor? Being able to influence students and alter lives was more rewarding than making money.

Of course, there were my failures—the Borlinda Borgias. Thank God, that girl hasn't been around for a few days to remind me. Still, I can't help wondering where she's at. The only time she had ever missed school was when she was performing in that religious epic for Maurice. Is it possible that she has accepted Maurice's generous offer and has decided to make more movies for Christ? I hope so. She really showed great promise, especially in that banquet scene.

After completing my cigarette, my gaze zoomed in on that same fair-haired man in the sunglasses and dark suit that I had seen yesterday. He was sitting in his white car, talking to someone on a phone. While he talked, I noticed police cars approach the school and park near the exits.

Concerned, I immediately got out of the Jag and hurried into the building. En route to the office to tell Pepe, I ran into Roger and told him about my conversation yesterday, and what I had just seen.

"Then what I've heard must be true," Roger said.

"What's that?"

"The Colombians have cut a deal with Borlinda."

"That man wasn't Colombian."

"That isn't what I mean, Frank. I'll explain it to you later. Now I've got to go and warn everyone."

I was searching the school for Pepe, when I heard a violent explosion. In the hall, not far from my class, the door to the science lab flew off its hinges and crashed against the wall. As I saw the cloud of smoke escape from the lab and fill the hall, I became concerned about the possibility of casualties. I turned to a boy nearby, and asked him to check the room for injuries, but he merely showed me a finger and hurried away.

Fortunately, the fire department found no bodies. The science students were cleaning the restrooms at the time. It amazed me how concerned these students were about the foul smells there. Cleaning the restrooms was really the custodians' responsibility. Yet this extraordinary group of young men and women took on the job themselves as a science project. It truly pleased me to know what a fine generation of children we had created. The fair-haired man in the sunglasses, who had arrived with a squad of police, was also impressed. On the other hand, seeing the science room in ashes, reduced to its masonry walls and concrete floor shocked him. When I looked in, they were probing through the remains for clues to the explosion. I overheard the man in sunglasses tell a policeman that the room looked as though it had been fire bombed. I told him that was impossible, and that the explosion was obviously caused by a gas leak, but he merely gave me a funny look and said, "Oh sure," then walked away.

After the excitement, I returned to my classroom. On my desk was a very thick envelope with my name on it. I opened it, and inside the envelope was a stack of hundred dollar bills. I wondered who was responsible. I knew my students were all very appreciative of my lectures, and from time to time, felt a need to modestly show their appreciation. But never with a bundle of tax-free dollars like this— seven hundred, eight hundred, nine hundred. . . .

Oh, how I love teaching. The joys, the rewards.

Pepe was very upset about the science room. Being the old friend that I was I gave up my free period to comfort him.

"You worry too much Pepe," I said. "You should be thrilled that the room was empty, and no one was hurt."

"Of course, you're right. Still, it is a little strange that all the kids were working on a science project at the time of the explosion—even the police thought so too."

"Forget the police, Pepe. They aren't paid to think. In fact, yesterday I told the one in the sunglasses exactly. . . ."

"You've talked to him yesterday?"

"You know how it is, Pepe. When you're as famous as I, you talk to all types of people all the time."

"Did you know that he's a narcotic agent?"

"Narcotic agent? Why would a narcotic agent come to our school? Everyone knows Horace Mann is in a drug-free zone."

"Well, that isn't what he heard. According to him, the pills produced in the science room are what's killing kids— not some mysterious virus. Imagine what a scandal that would be if it were ever proven true."

"Who could've given him such a crazy idea?"

"Borlinda."

"I should've guessed. Oh, the *grief* that girl causes! If I ever catch that little bitch, I'm going to grind her into a Polish sausage."

"That's not going to be easy—unless you want to search for her in the Amazon."

"The Amazon? What's she doing there?"

"Phyl told me—that her mother told her—that Borlinda has finally seen the Light, and has gone to Colombia as a Baptist missionary to save Colombians from Catholicism."

"I hope some boa constrictor has her for lunch. What nerve she has spreading such a lie about our school."

"That isn't all Phyl told me. According to Mrs. Borgia, Borlinda claims *full* responsibility for the faintings, which she brought about by chemically altering Roger's vitamins supply. It's supposed to be her way of punishing those kids (and especially Roger) for their sinful ways."

"That's too outrageous, even for Borlinda. Unless, of course, she's finally done it and gone over the deep end."

"Regardless, replacing the science room isn't going to be cheap. If the insurance company refuses to pay for any reason, the board could get fed up with me and do something awful." He then cringed. "Like throw me back into the classroom!"

"What's so awful about that?" I said, thinking about my Jaguar and tax-free cash gifts. "There are lots of rewards in teaching."

"Maybe for some. For me, I have a dream. Someday I want to go downtown and head the schools like Phyl. I can't afford to have problems like this. They don't look good on my résumé."

"Is there anything I can do?"

"Nothing, Frank," he said. *"Honest!* You've done so much already."

"But I want to do more."

He sighed. "That's what I fear."

That evening before retiring I turned on the television. Since my article appeared in *The Morning Meddler*, I watched all the major news shows. When you are in the limelight like me, thanks to my perceptive grasp of the problems in education, you become public property.

Oh, the scrutiny that goes with success!

But tonight's news had little to say about education. The ten o'clock only briefly mentioned the explosion at Horace Mann before switching to the headline story: the gangland slaying of Colombian drug dealers in an exclusive northshore suburb.

"Tonight at seven o'clock an explosion rocked the quiet suburb of Lake Wood. The explosion occurred at the home of Pedro Bolivar, a reputed kingpin for the Colombian drug cartel, while he was holding a meeting with his leading drug dealers to discuss new strategies for regaining control of the lucrative drug market in the city. Although no one knows for certainty how many died, most authorities agree that the explosion seriously weakened the Colombian drug trade by killing its main distributors. Unconfirmed reports indicate that a man by the name of Kelly Jones, who is linked with Washington, is responsible for the bombing."

Disgusted with all this violence, bored with all this talk about Colombian nationals, I quickly rose to shut off the television. You would think important things, like what I had to say about the faintings, would make the news. Who cares about some explosion at a Latin house party? Before I could turn off the television, the newscaster started talking about the teachers' reaction to a recent article on education. The minute I heard that I turned on my VCR to tape his report.

Oh, how thrilling. I'm going to make the ten o'clock!

I must call everyone and let them know. I'm sure Pepe, and the teachers will be *dying* to watch this. Maybe I should call Phyllis too?

Pepe's telephone line was busy, and so were the lines of several of the teachers I had tried. I decided to give up calling, figuring they were sending out the word themselves, and I turned my full attention to the television.

"City teachers," the newsman said, "furious with the tell-all article in *The Morning Meddler* early this week, responded with cries of protest, as they burned in effigy the author at a local teachers' union meeting tonight."

The camera, after catching a shot of the meeting, focused on Phyllis Jaffe. She was wearing a dress with painted flowers and a felt hat with artificial fruit. She reminded me, standing so tall and regal, of a hook-nose basketball player in drag, trying to imitate British royalty. "Tell me, Ms. Jaffe," the newsman asked, "what do you think about the teachers' reaction to the newspaper article in *The Morning Meddler?*"

The camera zoomed in for a close-up of her mannish face, and everyone paused in anticipation of the brilliant thought, which began to form on her lips. "Well, Ms. Jaffe," the man asked anxiously. "Your thoughts, please."

"*Oi vehy,*" she said succinctly to millions of listeners.

The news then switched to cover the city council election results. Disappointed, I turned off the television.

They didn't even mention my name. They could've at least mentioned my name. But no, they only give me a few moments of air time, and they never once identify me so the world will know who I am. *I hate the ten o'clock news!*

The next morning, when I arrived at school, the entire teaching staff paraded in front of the entrance, chanting, "Roast Hammy!" One teacher carried a poster of my family coat of arms with a pig's ass instead of a boar's head, while another had a poster of someone holding a tray with just a photograph of my head on it, and the headline "Save Our Children—Serve Your Family Hamme!" All of them looked hostile, ready to fight. Their fists were in the air, their voices loud and mean, as they chanted: "Roast *Hammy.*"

Opposing the teachers were a group of concerned citizens, carrying, "Hamme Makes Sense" signs. These concerned citizens who were all of Latin origin looked like oversized wrestlers and professional hit men. When their gazes locked with the teachers, they let it be known by their expressions that they would kill for their Hamme. A local television crew taped everything for the entire city to see on the Midday News. But their attention immediately turned to me when I got out of my car.

"There he is," one of the teachers shouted, pointing. "There's the loose nut."

The teachers circled me, chanting: "Roast Hammy, Roast Hammy!" Inside the circle with me were a cameraman and a television reporter. Before I realized what was happening, the camera was live, and a reporter was asking questions and shoving a microphone in my face for my response. As I was being taped, I could hear the verbal clash of citizens and teachers. "It isn't Frank who's the loose nut," an angry Latin hollered. "It's teachers like you by boring our kids with all that history 'n' stuff!"

"What are you? Some sort of moron?" a teacher hollered back. "Why are you sending your kid to school, if you don't want him to learn all that history 'n' stuff'?"

"Look-it-here-you-bitch, don't-you-call-me-no-moron!"

"If the shoe fits. . . ."

"Tell me, Mr. Hamme," the reporter asked. "Don't you feel you have been a little excessive in your criticisms of teachers?"

"I think not. In fact, their behavior right now demonstrates unequivocally their professional inadequacies. If they were truly professional with a commitment to their work, they wouldn't resort to such infantile protests. Instead, they would be more adult. Maybe write a scholarly article on the subject, or debate me, or perform other dignified activities rather than this embarrassing public display of anger."

"But wouldn't you be angry and wouldn't you protest openly if you were misquoted and held up for public ridicule by an article which you believed was just a. . .well, a *tad* inaccurate?"

"If that were the case, then that would only motivate me that much more to protest in an adult way. But obviously these teachers aren't capable of defending their questionable teaching practices in such a manner. For that reason, they must resort to infantile protests and, in the process, interrupt the education of the very students they claim they are dedicated to helping. It's all very unprofessional, very repugnant, and it reveals them for what they really are."

The reporter and the cameraman abruptly ended the interview and turned their attention to the teachers and citizens, when a fight broke out.

"Don't you push me!" one voice said.

"Then get that sign out of my face!" another responded

"Very well," an oversized Latin said, shoving his sign into the teacher's stomach. "Is that better?" he asked, as the teacher folded in pain.

Within moments, the teachers and concerned citizens were an angry entanglement of signs and bodies. I quickly entered the school. Being near this spectacle was quite distasteful. I truly loved teaching, and it tore my heart to see teachers reduced to this level.

Pepe was standing by the door, when I entered.

"This whole thing is getting out of hand, Frank," he said, upset. "What am I going to do? The teachers refuse to be cooperative. They said they want you fired. Nothing short of firing you will bring them back into the classroom. I don't want to do that, Frank. You know how I feel about you. But the President has a big political investment in this school, and having our school pulled into such a bitter struggle makes us all look bad, and it could even cost me my job! What am I going to do, Frank? This whole thing is becoming a nightmare."

"Don't worry, Pepe," I said, trying to comfort him. "It'll all blow over. Things like this always blow over in a few days. Trust me."

"I don't know, Frank. Too many things have happened— Mimi's death, the faintings, the science room, and now this. Why did it all have to happen at once? Why *here* of all places?"

I put my arm around him, comforting him like a man comforting a woman in distress. "Life's strange, Pepe. That's why we must be strong. We must hold our heads high and go forward and never yield to those forces trying to destroy us."

He just looked at me, speechless. What could he say to someone as courageous as I? All he could do was nod, then return to his office. Watching him leave, I felt a deep sorrow. I would've never written that article, if I had known it would have led to this. I was really only doing it for him. But it backfired, and now everything has changed.

What am I going to do? My oldest and dearest friend is in crisis, because of me. How can I change everything for him, short of quit? What can I do to help him and at the same time save my job? Certainly there must be a way of turning those teachers around and making them realize that my way is the *right* way!

But how?

As though this weren't enough, almost immediately after the explosion the students changed and lost all interest in school. They were restless and angry, some even sweaty and sickly. Nothing I said or did interested them. When they weren't complaining about the science room, they were pestering Roger for vitamins. But because of the tremendous demand for pills, and an unexpected reduction in supply, he was always out of stock, which, for some strange reason, deepened their anger toward what had happened to the science lab.

I have never witnessed anything like this in all my life. I must admit my first impressions of them last fall were wrong. They certainly aren't the apathetic students I thought they were. Instead, they turned out to be very caring, health-conscious young men and women with a strong regard for their school.

Because of all the excitement at school, only a few students came to class. Many of them lingered outside to watch the teachers and citizens exchange fists and expletives. Like the dedicated teacher that I was, I ignored this public display of bad taste and spent my morning in the classroom, pondering solutions. In the middle of a thought, Roger entered.

"You certainly infuriated those teachers," he said. "Not one wants to cross that picket line until you're fired."

"I know," I said, "and all because I told the truth."

"You should talk to them, Frank. With your golden tongue, you could easily persuade them to reconsider."

"It's too late for that, Roger. I think it's time they heard from someone else, someone more persuasive. Maybe it's time for the students to speak up."

Roger smiled. "Of course," and his face glowed, all white teeth and youthful good looks. "You're absolutely right, Frank. Why didn't I think of that myself? They obviously need something more than a little muscle from a few of my tough Latin friends. It's time for *real* action. Just leave it to me, and those teachers will be kissing your ass."

"Well, I wasn't thinking of having them go that far?"

"I'm sure you weren't," he said, winking. He then gave me one of his hand-rolled cigarettes, and watched me greedily smoke it. "Well, I've got to go. My supplier has just gotten in a shipment of generic vitamins, and I want to get my share before they're all sold out."

Despite the teachers' blatant disapproval of my article, I still managed to succeed where many had failed. Because of the importance of what I had to say, I was able to achieve a larger good and, in the process, create for myself an opportunity to discuss good teaching practices. Reporters, interested in my views, continuously asked me questions about everything, from what I thought teachers should be paid to how popular subjects should be taught. Even the local university took an interest in me and asked me to hold a faculty seminar on how to use hypnotism to teach literature.

Thanks to Roger, everything changed at school for me as well. This remarkable young man was so committed to helping me that he refused to sell his generic vitamins to any teacher (and student) who didn't return to class and show a little more kindness toward me. His appeal on my behalf was so persuasive, according to rumors, that *some* of the teachers and students became even a little militant in my defense. It was said privately that they punctured auto tires, threatened lives, and even blackened a few eyes of anyone who showed any hostility toward me. Whatever the truth (and I deeply question such *extreme* behavior from anyone at Horace Mann High) Roger was so successful at winning the support of his health-conscious student and teacher customers that the faculty after brief deliberation not only wanted me to remain on the staff, but they also wanted me to be their *director of education!* Of course, I leaped at the opportunity. As the director of education, I would have the chance to plan the curriculum and introduce those wonderful courses I had dreamed about (like "Famous Nymphomaniacs and Pedophiles in History" and "Learning Slang in French, German and Spanish.")

When Phyllis Jaffe learned about my success, she phoned me to compliment me on my skill at influencing the teachers to return to class, and she called my article "one of the best damn pieces of journalism she has ever read." Even the President's wife congratulated me "for having the courage to take on the educational establishment and the strength to tame it with such bold thinking."

But the crowning point came, when I was finally acknowledged as a superteacher and was chosen *teacher of the year!* My article for *The Morning Meddler*, my success at teaching Roger Murphy, and my influence with the teachers and students all contributed to persuading the committee that I was the *best* example in the entire country of a *good* teacher!

Because of the importance of the award, the President's wife volunteered to make the presentation to me in person. Even the editor of the prestigious *American Public School Journal for the Affirmation of Pedagogic Integrity* agreed to attend the presentation He was so thrilled to publish such an original piece on Chaucer that he shuttled here from New York just so that he could meet and talk with me about doing a column for his publication.

As though all this weren't enough, the science wing was completed in record time. Rather than wait for the insurance to pay (after months of tiresome investigation) and for the school system to get around to contracting the job (after the usual bureaucratic delays), Roger volunteered to finance it himself. It was his gesture of love toward a school that made him the special person he was, and for the many teachers (namely me) who so unselfishly gave so much of themselves to helping him realize his potential.

No money was spared in rebuilding the science lab. All the latest technology was used, including an alarm system with camera surveillance, and a sophisticated ventilation system to clear the room quickly of foul smelling odors. For absolute safety, a laser monitoring system was installed to scan the room. At the touch of a remote control button, it would efficiently destroy any hazardous waste. In appreciation for his generosity, the school board agreed to contract with Roger to handle the maintenance.

Thanks to my efforts and influence, a truly Renaissance school was taking shape. Rising from the ashes of antiquated teaching practices and curricula, soaring gloriously like a Phoenix into the heaven, was a new view of education. As I stood in the wings of the stage, staring through the opening in the curtain at all the educators, parents, students, and reporters who came to see me, I felt an enormous pride in my contribution. Soon I would be presented to the world. Television cameras and reporters would record this moment for history. Through the miracle of satellite communications I would be introduced to America (*the world!*) as the *best* public school teacher of the year—and as the man who single-handedly was changing the way we viewed education.

Sitting off stage surrounded by the secret service was the President's wife. I wanted to introduce myself, but hesitated. She was eating a slice of chocolate, raspberry cake with whipped cream. Since I knew what a magnificent effect, it had on her intellectually, I thought it would be prudent to wait until later. It was obvious by her expression while eating the cake that she was going to be brilliant. After licking the plate clean, she started to grab for another piece, but was stopped by a man who quickly removed it. A violent look crossed her face, which would have terrified most men, but, which didn't even phase him.

"Later," he said politely. "Now you must get ready for your entrance. Remember, *the country needs you!*"

"Thank you, Adolf, for reminding me," she said, rising majestically, like an elderly, anorectic-looking aristocrat.

After she disappeared with her security men, my gaze zoomed in on the unguarded chocolate cake, and I felt a tremendous desire for a slice. When no one was looking, I cut myself a piece with my fingers; then, hiding behind a curtain, I greedily ate it. Almost immediately after finishing it my body began to tingle and lighten, and *scream* for more cake. Pretending to be practicing a new dance step, I moved toward the cake, and, when no one was looking, I grabbed the entire cake, then with one grand leap disappeared behind the curtain.

Before the house lights dimmed, I peeked between the curtains at all my friends in the audience who came to witness this auspicious moment. There was Pepita wearing an elegant black dress and a single strand of pearls. Next to her was the man she loved, looking like a bear in a sports jacket and sport shirt, holding her dainty hand in his huge hairy paw. Then there was the bullish Phyllis Jaffe wearing a navy blue pants suit and Salvador-Dalí tie. She was sitting next to a stunning blonde woman in a red suit who had a remarkable resemblance to a middle-aged Borlinda. The two women were politely talking and reading to each other from the Bible.

Near the entrance, I saw Roger in an Uncle Sam costume, selling vitamins. Although Phyllis never rescinded her order against conducting business in the school, she did make an exception in Roger's case, because of the proven health benefits of vitamins (and his generous donation of a science lab). Of course, like a greedy loan shark's daughter, she did demand a fifty percent cut of his profits, which she split with the police department to help combat crime. I thought her demands were excessive, and told Roger so, but he disagreed. He felt that it was all for a good cause and, like everyone else, he was generally happy with the arrangement. In fact, I have never seen my students so happy, as they were now, popping vitamins, while eagerly awaiting for me to appear. Seeing them and the faculty (who have become my *closest* and *dearest* friends) brought joy to my heart. This great moment could never have been possible if I hadn't had the courage to tell the truth.

As I stood there, observing the audience from behind the curtain, the house lights dimmed and the orchestra began to play a medley of patriotic tunes. Knocking into me, dressed in red, white and blue, were the singers hurrying on stage for their opening number. As I spun on my heel like a top, ready to lose my balance from all the bumping, the orchestra finished the medley, and at the exact moment they finished, I fell on my ass on the stage with the cake crushed in my hand. To hide me and save me for my grand entrance, the singers stepped over me while someone dragged me off stage from behind.

The moment the curtain was parted, the stage exploded with bright lights and color. A chorus of red, white, and blue patriots, marching in place, began to rejoice in song the thrill of being an American. After singing their tribute to America and Americans, the singers parted in the center. A single soft spot hit center stage and illuminated the President's wife who through the miracle of makeup and costume was transformed into a Statue of Liberty. Behind her was a backdrop of flags from around the world. While the stage lighted up like a Fourth of July fireworks display, the chorus sang, "Hail to the Chief's wife."

It was a splendid entrance, and to make certain everyone properly appreciated it, a man offstage played a tape of whistles and applause. After a few minutes of whistles and applause, the President's wife made a gesture with her hand to quiet the audience, and the tape was immediately shut off. The singers silently disappeared from the stage, and left it for the President's wife to command.

I turned to the man who had played the tape, and I asked him if he would also do the same for me. Instead of replying, obviously unaware of who I was, he merely laughed, then turned away and began to smoke an aromatic herbal cigarette. I decided to teach him a lesson and give him a good kick, but when I lifted my leg, I misjudged his location and kicked a secret service man instead. At that moment, I was whisked away by some rough-looking stagehand who, after dropping me in a corner, told me to behave.

"My dear friends," the Statue of Liberty began, "you just don't know how thrilled I am to be at Horace Mann today, and to present the most coveted award in teaching to one of your very own teachers. As my dear husband has so often said on the campaign trail, 'education is the single most important program our government sponsors.' That's why he has risked his political career by redirecting monies intended for military defense, as well as judicial and penal reform to education. Ladies and gentlemen, I am proud to announce that the President of the United States is officially making available on this day enough funds to implement in every major city in America a Renaissance high school just like Horace Mann." (The applause and whistles began again, and this time they lasted for two minutes.) "And to Horace Mann High," she continued, "for its remarkable achievement in education, he is giving a special $5 million grant for financing a program that your new director of education will implement next term." (This time the whistles and applause lasted a record *five* minutes!)

"To accept this award, I would like your very own principal, Mr. Pepe Noriega. . . ." she paused, cleared her throat. "I mean Ms. Pepita Noriega to step up here."

Pepita wiggled herself free of Niko, then glided across the stage. "Thank you, Ms. Wilson. On behalf of the teaching staff, the student body, the community—and especially the staff of the Edmund Park Hotel who always so graciously provides us with such a magnificent setting for our faculty *soirées*—we would like to give you and the President our kindest thanks. You can be certain that this money will be spent in a manner that will benefit everyone associated with Horace Mann—especially my wonderful fiancé, Niko Papalodopoulos, and all our dedicated faculty members and students." She then blew Niko a kiss and glided from the stage with the check pressed against her ample breasts.

"Thank you, Ms. Noriega," the Statue of Liberty said. "I want you all to know that if my husband is reelected again next term, he will continue his generous support of education."

She then told them his dream to create full-service schools and mentioned some of my ideas—longer school days, nursery facilities, medical staffing, and other services to meet the needs of modern America twelve hours a day and twelve months a year! She talked untiringly about her husband and the reelection campaign, and all the wonderful things he has done and will continue to do for education if he is reelected.

Dressed in my cap and gown, I stood in front of a little red school house backdrop and wondered how much longer I will have to wait before that bitch introduces me. The most important moment of my life, in which every cell in my body was gaily celebrating, was being ruined by a long-winded hag. If she weren't the President's wife (and so carefully protected by the secret service), I would've yanked her off stage a long time ago.

She must've sensed my anger, because she suddenly stopped promoting her husband and her great dream for American kids, and she came directly to the point—*me!*

"The media say so many unkind things about the schools," she continued in what sounded like the voice of an angel. "But that's because until now they haven't had the privilege of meeting one of your teachers. This man with his brilliant article in *The Morning Meddler* has succeeded at proving that education, when done well, can achieve beyond expectations. By being a maverick, and challenging established views, he has succeeded singly at changing the way we think about education. Dear ladies and gentlemen, I want you to meet the man who is bringing a true Renaissance to

American education. I want you to meet Horace Mann's very own, Frank Hamme, *teacher of the year!"*

After finishing the cake and licking the chocolate from each finger, I stood there listening, overcome by excitement. At the exact moment when the bitch finally shut up and the blinding light hit me, every cell in my body clinked champagne glasses in honor of this moment. As I stared in awe into the warm embrace of that spot, mesmerized by its brilliance, I began to feel myself slowly lift and dissolve into the Light. What could I say during this great moment? How could I ever find the right words to express my thrill? I was experiencing what only one man had ever experienced. In front of all my students and friends—and for the entire world to see on television—I, *Frank Hamme, was being transfigured!*

What a moment! *What a moment!*

A voice came toward me from no where in particular and everywhere in general. "It is with great honor that I present to you the Golden Apple Award in appreciation for your many contributions to teaching." A bright, gold apple floated toward me. I leaped forward to grab it and, in the process, knocked the Statue of Liberty into a dark abyss. As it fell screaming, I clutched the apple and held it to the Light. At that exact moment, when the apple was clutched in my hands, I felt myself become one with the Light.

As I spoke, I heard my words drift slowly into space, echoing and reechoing until they disappeared into the vast universe. *"To all of you out there, To all of you out there, To all of you out there. . . ."*

As I spoke, I made every effort to be brief and eloquent. I never mentioned once any of the teachers who had tried to corrupt me with thinking skills or to restrain my natural impulses with threats or to tarnish my grasp of the classics with reason. Instead, I addressed only the positive forces in my life and identified the important teachers, programs, schools that made this moment possible. I thanked everyone by name and deed who helped create me into the unique person I was. I reminisced over some of my students who have gone on to achieve, their intimate thoughts they shared with me, their special talents I nurtured. But most of all, I talked about our wonderful country, America, the melting pot of the world, where (thanks to the public schools) we were all learning to live together harmoniously.

When I finished speaking, heaven opened up and all the angels rejoiced together and sang "America." Gazing into the blinding light, an omnipresent voice whispered to me, "Today, Frank, teacher of the year. Tomorrow, *Secretary of Education!*"

Excellent!

Author

Joe David taught for about 14 years in public and private schools in the East. Concerned about what was happening in education, he began to write about his observations. Many of his views, which were developing while teaching, became the themes for his articles, columns and books.

His first book, *The Fire Within*, because of its successful dramatization of important education philosophies, made the reading list at two universities and received national public attention. For about nine years, Mr. David was a frequent radio and television talk show guest who candidly discussed issues in education. His lively, on-air conversations with enthusiastic audiences became the basis for his second book, *Glad You Asked!* Over the years, he has written for professional journals, newspapers, magazines, newsletters and books, including the Annenberg/CPB Math and Science Project, *Education Magazine*, *The Forum* (University of West Florida), and *Basic Education* (Council for Basic Education).

The Fire Within

A violence-ridden school is the setting for Joe David's hard look into the world of "education," a world filled with hatred and deception, boredom and indoctrination, generously financed by government decree. The central character is Anne Harte, an idealist who teaches by igniting the fire within for knowledge. Unlike other teachers who indoctrinate, Anne is committed to teaching her students to think. Her commitment to reason places her in direct conflict with the system. Representing the system, and modern "education," is Loretta Daniels, the principal. Unlike Anne, Loretta believes children must "satisfy their needs, their instincts and impulses by action." What results is a fast-paced look at "education" with Loretta and Anne fighting for the survival of their diametric philosophies. In the background are the victims—and one especially angry victim, a teenage thug who is determined to rape Anne.

Glad You Asked!

Documented, pensive, paced, *Glad You Asked!* by Joe David, is a primary source book for those needing to know about public education. Based on questions most often asked the author during radio and television appearances, *Glad You Asked!* is about a public school scandal that renders children intellectually useless and morally bankrupt. It is also about a common-sense approach to educational survival: *good* teaching, *good* education, and the *right* way to protect children from the intellectual lobotomy of educationists.

For a copy of *Glad You Asked!* and *The Fire Within,* contact:
Books For All Times, Inc.
P.O. Box 2
Alexandria, VA 22313
http://www.bfat.com